# Chocolat

ERIC LANLARD

Photography by Kate Whitaker

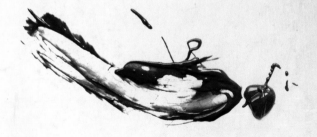

# Chocolat

### SEDUCTIVE RECIPES FOR BAKED GOODS, DESSERTS, TRUFFLES, AND OTHER TREATS

**ERIC LANLARD**

Photography by Kate Whitaker

MITCHELL BEAZLEY

*To Paul and Bobby, for their continuous support.*

First published in Great Britain in 2013 by Mitchell Beazley,
an imprint of Octopus Publishing Group Ltd,
Endeavour House, 189 Shaftesbury Avenue,
London WC2H 8JY
www.octopusbooks.co.uk

An Hachette UK Company
www.hachette.co.uk

Distributed in the US by Hachette Book Group USA
237 Park Avenue, New York NY 10017 USA

Distributed in Canada by Canadian Manda Group
165 Dufferin Street, Toronto, Ontario, Canada M6K 3H6

**Publisher** Alison Starling
**Art direction and design** Juliette Norsworthy
**Senior editor** Sybella Stephens
**Home economists** Rachel Wood, Wendy Lee
**Photography** Kate Whitaker
**Prop stylist** Liz Belton
**Production** Caroline Alberti

ISBN: 978 1 84533 788 9
Printed and bound in China

Large eggs and whole milk should be used,
unless otherwise stated.

# Contents

# Introduction

At the age of ten, my attraction to chocolate—the "food of the gods"—had already started. In fact, my memories go much farther back to my family's daily visits to the local boulangerie in France, where we would buy a brioche and a single bar of dark "Chocolat Poulain"—the trick was to push the bar up without breaking it and enjoy it on the way to school. The reason that, years later, I chose Le Grand Pâtisserie in Quimper for my apprenticeship is because it was the only local boutique that made its own chocolate!

My fascination with this precious ingredient is still with me, and over the years I have made it my mission to discover the history and origins of chocolate, and the techniques of its production. To understand the whole process, from cocoa bean to an indulgent, finished product, I have been lucky enough to walk through a fertile hacienda in South America and a plantation in Trinidad to touch, taste, and smell the raw ingredient, and then witness the long process of the cocoa beans being roasted, conched, blended, and molded into delicious chocolate bars, eggs, or other fabulous shapes.

However, as much as I adore eating chocolate, it's as a baking ingredient that I love it the most, and with this new book, I want to share my passion for chocolate with you. From indulgent chocolate drinks, tarts, muffins, and mousses to gâteaux, petits fours, and elaborate creations for special occasions, join me in the madness of baking with chocolate!

*Eric* x

# A brief history of chocolate

Originating in the rain forests of Central America, the cacao tree was first cultivated as early as 1500 BC by the Olmecs, followed later by the Maya and Aztec peoples, who enjoyed a beverage called *chocolati* (bitter water). The drink was made by roasting and crushing cocoa beans on a hot stone, then the rich paste was mixed into hot water with the addition of vanilla, pepper, cinnamon, and anise. It was enjoyed as a nourishing, power-busting drink and aphrodisiac. The Maya and Aztec peoples also used the precious beans as money—taxes and slave transactions were paid and made with cocoa beans.

In 1519, the conquistador Hernán Cortés reached modern-day Mexico and began the conquest of that country. The Aztec emperor Montezuma gave Cortés a cup of freshly prepared cocoa, who later wrote: "After drinking this elixir you could just go on and on and travel the world without fatigues and without need for other food." In 1524, Cortés sent Charles I of Spain a cargo of cocoa beans and the King of Spain and his court enjoyed the delights of this precious ingredient, adding honey to it to make it sweeter. Spain kept its monopoly of the cocoa trade for years until it started to appear all over Europe during the seventeenth century, especially in Italy, France, and Great Britain.

As chocolate grew more popular, the way to treat it became more sophisticated, with new techniques and machinery introduced, but it wasn't until 1802 that the Italians fully industrialized chocolate production.

Milk chocolate was first made by a Swiss named Daniel Peter in 1875, and his compatriot Rodolphe Lindt invented the conching process to refine the texture of chocolate, which revolutionized the way chocolate is made and eaten.

## The production process

My favorite treat begins its life inside a cocoa bean, which grow on trees in the tropics of West Africa, Southeast Asia, and South America (the best varieties are grown on small family farms or haciendas)—the cocoa beans, from which chocolate is made, are the seeds of the cacao tree found within the bean.

The cocoa beans are harvested and taken to cooperatives, where they are opened. The seeds and pulp are scooped out, then fermented and dried. The cocoa beans are then taken abroad to be processed. The dried beans, like coffee, are roasted and crushed, then the husks are removed and the cocoa nibs are pressed through rollers to make "chocolate liquor." After more pressing, the combination of cooling and heating processes, and the addition of sugar and other ingredients, the final precious product runs free from the heavy machinery and is then transformed into bars, disks, and chips, ready to be eaten or used in baking.

# Know your chocolate

## How to choose a good chocolate

Choosing a good chocolate is first a question of taste. In its raw state, cacao is bitter, so the taste and quality of chocolate depends on the percentage of cocoa solids it contains, the provenance of the cocoa beans, and the production process. A good-quality chocolate has a shiny finish and is brittle, with a strong characteristic taste and smoothness, and it should not stick to the palate.

A premium chocolate will also have mostly cocoa butter as its main fat content. For baking or making desserts, I personally like to use chocolate with a maximum of 70 percent cocoa solids, because chocolate with a higher percentage of cocoa solids can be too bitter.

## Storing chocolate

Avoid storing chocolate in the refrigerator—keep it in a cool (60–70°F), dry, and dark place, away from the strong odors of spices, strong foods, or other cooking smells.

If your chocolate has a white discoloration on its surface (chocolate bloom), it is best to discard it, because that means it is old or has been stored in extreme temperatures.

# Working with chocolate

## Melting chocolate

### In a bain-marie

The classic way to melt chocolate is the bain-marie, or water-bath, method. Put the chopped-up chocolate in a heatproof bowl set over a saucepan of barely simmering water. For a great result, the secret is to melt the chocolate gently over very low heat, making sure the surface of the water does not touch the bottom of the bowl. If you have a double boiler, you can use it instead of the bowl over the saucepan.

### In a microwave

Alternatively, you can put the chopped-up chocolate into a microwavable bowl and zap it in the microwave on high power for a few seconds at a time, stirring gently in between bursts, until melted. Every microwave is different, so first test a small amount of chocolate in your microwave to see how long it takes to melt. Remember, milk and white chocolates burn more easily than dark chocolate, so be cautious and gentle when melting them, whichever process you use.

# Tempering chocolate

### What is tempering?

Tempering is a technique that pastry chefs and chocolatiers use to stabilize chocolate and achieve a glossy, hard, brittle finish, making tempered chocolate perfect for dipping individual chocolates and truffles or coating cookies and cakes. It involves melting and cooling chocolate, then bringing it to the correct temperature for coating.

### The technique

For best results, use a chocolate or candy thermometer to check that the correct temperature for each stage has been reached.

First, if using a bar of chocolate, chop your chocolate as finely as possible. Melt two-thirds of it in a heatproof bowl set over a saucepan of barely simmering water (see Melting Chocolate on page 11). Remove the bowl from the pan when the chocolate is just melted and has reached the required temperature (see the chart on the facing page). Add the remaining chocolate a little at the time, stirring gently between additions. Continue to stir gently until all the chocolate is melted and the mixture has cooled to 79–81°F (see the chart on the facing page).

Return the bowl of melted chocolate to the pan and reheat to 82–86°F (see the chart on the facing page). To test, drizzle a few drops of the chocolate onto a piece of parchment paper; the chocolate should set in a few minutes and be ready for use. If it sets too fast, return the bowl to the pan and heat for a few seconds to make it more fluid. Use for dipping and coating.

## Chocolate Tempering Temperatures

| Chocolate | Melted Temperature | Cooled Temperature | Reheated Temperature |
|-----------|--------------------|--------------------|----------------------|
| Dark | 122°F | 81°F | 86°F |
| Milk | 113°F | 81°F | 84°F |
| White | 104°F | 79°F | 82°F |

Chocolate and vanilla marble cake

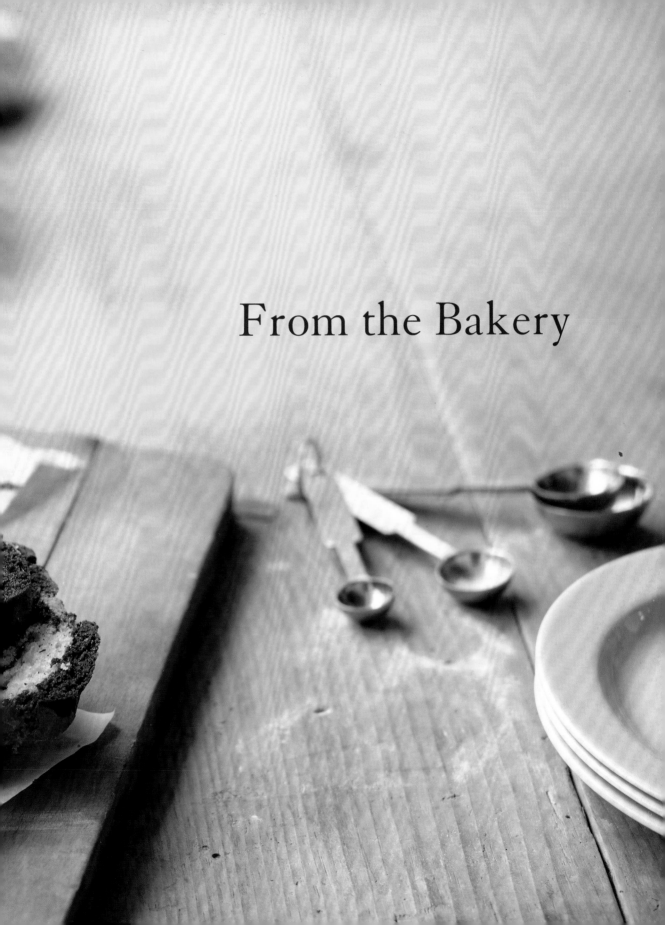

From the Bakery

# Chocolate and vanilla marble cake

This recipe is one of my earliest baking recipes. I used to make it every Wednesday when I was off school—it's fun and easy to make, and a great afternoon treat.

**Serves 8**

**Preparation time:** 15 minutes, plus cooling

**Cooking time:** 50 minutes

1 stick unsalted butter, melted and cooled, plus extra for greasing

4 ounces semisweet chocolate, coarsely chopped

5 eggs, separated

⅔ cup superfine sugar

1 cup all-purpose flour

2 teaspoons baking powder

2 teaspoons vanilla extract or paste

Preheat the oven to 350°F. Grease a 9 × 5 × 3-inch loaf pan and line with parchment paper.

Melt the chocolate in a heatproof bowl set over a saucepan of barely simmering water, making sure the surface of the water does not touch the bowl.

In a large bowl, beat together the egg yolks and sugar until pale, using an electric hand mixer. Beat in the cooled, melted butter, then sift in the flour and baking powder and fold in.

Separate the batter into two large bowls. Fold the vanilla into one of the bowls and the melted chocolate into the other. In a large, clean, dry bowl, whisk the egg whites to stiff peaks, then gently fold half of the egg whites into each cake batter.

Spoon layers of the batter alternately into the prepared pan, then run through a toothpick or skewer two or three times to create a marbled effect. Bake in the oven for 45 minutes, or until a toothpick inserted into the center comes out clean. Let cool in the pan for 10 minutes, then turn out onto a cooling rack to cool completely. See previous page for finished result.

## Tip

To make the cake even more luxurious, coat it with melted dark chocolate.

**1.** Beat together the egg yolks and sugar until pale.

**2.** Beat in the melted butter, then fold in the flour and baking powder.

**3.** Divide between two bowls and add the melted chocolate to one bowl.

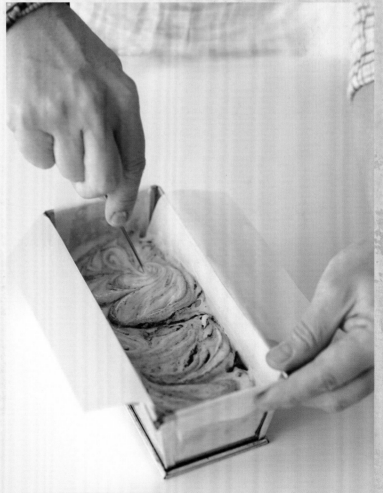

**4.** Make sure both the vanilla and chocolate are thoroughly mixed in.

**5.** Divide the whisked egg whites between the two bowls and gently fold in.

**6.** Alternately spoon the dark and light batters into the pan and run a toothpick or skewer through the them to create the marbled effect.

# Chocolate and cinnamon rolls

When I travel to the United States, I always make a point of going to the local bakery or food hall to get some freshly baked cinnamon rolls. The aroma is so spicy, sweet, and enticing. I like them dripping with icing, and these, of course, include my other favorite ingredient—chocolate!

**Makes 11**

**Preparation time:** 30 minutes, plus rising

**Cooking time:** 25–30 minutes

2 cups warm milk

¾ cup sugar

2 (⅔-ounce) cakes fresh yeast or 4½ teaspoons (2 envelopes) active dry yeast

1¾ sticks unsalted butter, melted, plus extra for greasing

2 teaspoons vanilla paste or extract

1 egg, plus 1 egg, beaten

8 cups all-purpose flour, plus extra for dusting

**For the filling**

3 ounces semisweet chocolate, grated

1 stick unsalted butter, melted and cooled

1 cup firmly packed dark brown sugar

3 tablespoons ground cinnamon

**For the glaze**

⅔ cup confectioners' sugar

1 teaspoon vanilla extract

1 tablespoon water

Start by making the dough. Put the milk, sugar, yeast, melted butter, vanilla, and whole egg into the bowl of a freestanding mixer fitted with a dough hook, then mix together until smooth. Sift the flour, then gradually add to the bowl, mixing until the dough comes away from the side of the bowl. Place the dough in a large, lightly floured bowl and cover with plastic wrap or a damp dish towel. Let rise for 45 minutes–1 hour at room temperature, or until the dough has almost doubled in volume.

To make the filling, beat the grated chocolate, cooled melted butter, sugar, and cinnamon in a bowl to a smooth, spreadable paste and put to one side.

When the dough has risen, punch it down to release the air, then turn out onto a lightly floured surface. Roll out the dough to a ½-inch thick rectangle, about 11 x 27 inches. Using a spatula, spread the filling all over the dough. Starting at a long edge, roll the dough into a long log shape without stretching it. Using a sharp knife, cut into slices about 2½ inches wide. Place them on two greased and floured baking sheets. Cover with plastic wrap or a damp dish towel and let rise for 30 minutes.

Preheat the oven to 400°F. Meanwhile, add the water to the beaten egg to make an egg wash. Use a pastry brush and lightly brush the tops of the rolls with the egg wash.

Bake the rolls in the oven for 10 minutes, then reduce the heat to 350°F and cook for another 15–20 minutes, or until golden brown, cooked in the center, and the rolls sound hollow when tapped on the bottoms.

Meanwhile, to make the glaze, mix together the confectioners' sugar, vanilla, and water in a bowl. As soon as the rolls are cooked, brush them generously with the glaze and let cool. These are fantastic served with coffee or hot chocolate.

# Pain au chocolat

After the croissant, the pain au chocolat is probably the most popular breakfast food in France. I certainly grew up eating these lovely flaky pastries on my way to school. This recipe requires you to wake up a little early to make them, but it's worth it, especially for a weekend treat.

**Makes 6**

**Preparation time:** 40 minutes, plus rising and chilling

**Cooking time:** 25–30 minutes

1 cup warm milk

1 teaspoon active dry yeast

1¼ sticks unsalted butter, plus extra for greasing

3 tablespoons granulated sugar

1 teaspoon salt

3⅔ cups all-purpose flour, sifted, plus extra for dusting

8 ounces semisweet chocolate, broken into 12 lengths

1 egg, beaten

Put the milk, yeast, 1 tablespoon of the butter, the sugar, and salt into the bowl of a freestanding mixer fitted with a dough hook, then mix well. Gradually add the flour, mixing until the dough comes away from the side of the bowl. Place the dough in a lightly floured bowl and cover with plastic wrap or a damp dish towel. Let rise for 40 minutes at room temperature, or until the dough has almost doubled in volume.

Using a rolling pin, lightly beat the remaining butter between two sheets of wax paper to a rectangle, 5 x 8 inches, and chill.

When the dough has risen, punch it down to release the air, then turn out onto a floured surface. Roll out the dough to a rectangle, 8 x 16 inches. Remove the butter from the wax paper and place in the center of the dough. Fold the dough over the butter like an envelope, making sure none of the butter is exposed.

Roll out the dough to an even rectangle, 8 x 20 inches. Fold the dough in thirds lengthwise, like a business letter. This completes the first turn. Rotate by 90 degrees so that the folded edge is on your left and the dough faces you like a book. Roll out again to a neat rectangle, 8 x 20 inches, and repeat the folding process. This completes the second turn. Cover with plastic wrap and chill in the refrigerator for at least 30 minutes. Repeat the process so that you end up with four turns in total, then chill for another 30 minutes.

Roll out the dough on a floured surface to a ¼-inch thick rectangle, 8 x 24 inches, then cut into six strips, about 4 x 8 inches. Place two strips of chocolate across the shorter length of a dough strip and roll up, enclosing the chocolate. Repeat with the remaining chocolate and dough strips. Place seam side down on a greased baking sheet and flatten them gently with your hand. Cover with plastic wrap and let rise at room temperature for 35–40 minutes.

Preheat the oven to 350°F. Brush the pastries with the beaten egg and bake in the oven for 25–30 minutes, or until golden brown. Let cool before serving.

# Devilish chocolate brownies

I know there are plenty of brownie recipes around, but this is my favorite dark chocolate version, and, of course, you can add nuts or dried fruits, if you want. Remember, don't overcook them.

**Makes 16**

**Preparation time:** 10 minutes

**Cooking time:** 30 minutes

8 ounces semiseweet chocolate, coarsely chopped

1¼ sticks unsalted butter, plus extra for greasing

2 teaspoons vanilla paste or extract

¾ cup granulated sugar

3 eggs, beaten

⅔ cup all-purpose flour

2 tablespoons unsweetened cocoa powder

1 teaspoon salt

⅔ cup semisweet chocolate chips

Preheat the oven to 350°F. Grease an 8-inch-square shallow baking pan and line the bottom with parchment paper.

Melt the chopped chocolate and butter with the vanilla in a heatproof bowl set over a saucepan of barely simmering water, making sure the surface of the water does not touch the bowl. Remove from the heat and stir in the sugar, then let cool for a few minutes.

Beat in the eggs, sift in the flour, cocoa, and salt, and fold in until the batter is smooth and glossy. Stir in he chocolate chips.

Pour the batter into the prepared pan and level the top. Bake in the oven for 25 minutes, or until the top starts to crack but the center remains gooey. Turn off the oven and keep the brownies inside the oven for another 5 minutes before removing. Let cool completely in the pan.

Cut the brownies into 16 small squares and remove from the pan. Store in an airtight container for up to 4 days.

# Chocolate Kouign Amann

Kouign Amann is a speciality from my native Brittany—it was invented by a pâtissier in the city of Douarnenez. The translation of the Breton name is "butter cake" and you will understand why when making it. This is my chocolate version.

**Serves 12**

**Preparation time:** 45 minutes, plus chilling and rising

**Cooking time:** 25–30 minutes

6 tablespoons unsalted butter, plus extra for greasing

1 teaspoon active dry yeast

⅓ cup warm water

1⅔ cups all-purpose flour, plus extra for dusting

1 teaspoon salt

1 stick salted butter

¾ cup granulated sugar

2 ounces semisweet chocolate, grated

Melt 4 tablespoons of the unsalted butter in a small saucepan. Put the yeast into a bowl and dissolve in the water, then mix in the melted butter.

Sift together the flour and salt into a large bowl. Make a well in the center, add the yeast mixture, and gradually mix together to form a dough. Turn out onto a floured surface and knead the dough for 10 minutes, until smooth and elastic. Cover with plastic wrap and chill in the refrigerator for at least 30 minutes.

Using a rolling pin, lightly beat the salted butter between two sheets of wax paper to form a rectangle, 5 x 8 inches. Place in the refrigerator with the dough.

Roll out the dough on a lightly floured surface to a 12-inch circle. Place the chilled butter in the center, then sprinkle over one-quarter of the sugar and grated chocolate. Fold the dough over the butter like an envelope, making sure none of the butter is exposed. Beat the dough slightly with the rolling pin, then roll out to an even rectangle, 8 x 16 inches.

Using a pastry brush, remove any flour from the dough. Fold the dough in thirds lengthwise, like a business letter. This completes the first turn. Rotate by 90 degrees so that the folded edge is on your left and the dough faces you like a book. Roll out again to a neat rectangle, 8 x 16 inches. Sprinkle over another quarter of the sugar and chocolate and repeat the folding process. This completes the second turn. Cover with plastic wrap and chill in the refrigerator for 30 minutes. Repeat the process, then cover and chill for another 30 minutes.

Preheat the oven to 400°F. Grease and flour a 12-inch-square baking pan.

Roll out the dough on a floured surface to a 12-inch square. Fold each corner into the middle and turn upside down into the pan. Melt the remaining unsalted butter in a saucepan, then brush liberally over the top. Sprinkle with the remaining sugar and chocolate. Let rise at room temperature for 25 minutes.

Bake in the oven for 25–30 minutes, or until golden and caramelized. Remove from the pan before completely cool, because the caramel will stick. This is best eaten hot with a traditional little glass of local Calvados, or in your case … apple brandy.

# White chocolate and lemon madeleines

Madeleines have had a huge revival recently, mostly as petits fours in restaurants. I prefer them full size, because they don't dry out so quickly. These chocolate versions will keep well in an airtight container or cookie jar.

**Makes 36**
**Preparation time:** 15 minutes
**Cooking time:** 35 minutes

2⅓ cups all-purpose flour, plus extra for dusting

4 ounces white chocolate, coarsely chopped

4 eggs

1 cup plus 2 tablespoons superfine sugar or granulated sugar

1 stick unsalted butter, plus extra for greasing

1½ teaspoons baking powder

grated zest of 1 lemon

Preheat the oven to 350°F. Grease and lightly flour a 12-cup madeleine pan.

Melt the butter and chocolate in a heatproof bowl set over a saucepan of barely simmering water, making sure the surface of the water does not touch the bowl. Let cool for a few minutes.

In a large bowl, beat together the eggs and sugar, using an electric handheld mixer, for several minutes, until pale and foamy, then beat in the cooled butter and chocolate mixture. Sift the flour and baking powder together, then gently fold into the mixture. Beat in the lemon zest until the batter is smooth and glossy.

Spoon the batter into the cups of the prepared pan, filling them three-quarters full. Bake in the oven for 10 minutes, or until light golden. Transfer immediately to a cooling rack. Repeat with the remaining batter.

## Tip

Use low heat to melt white chocolate, because it can burn very easily.

# Mini red velvet cakes with white chocolate frosting

This all-American favorite is now a worldwide sensation, and the use of oil and buttermilk make it extremely moist. My twist on the frosting makes this version even more indulgent.

**Makes 6**

**Preparation time:** 40 minutes, plus cooling

**Cooking time:** 40 minutes

butter, for greasing

1 cup plus 2 tablespoons granulated sugar

2 eggs

scant 1¼ cups vegetable oil

½ cup buttermilk

1 tablespoon red food coloring

1 teaspoon vanilla extract

1⅓ cups all-purpose flour

3 tablespoons unsweetened cocoa powder

½ teaspoon baking powder

½ teaspoon salt

2 teaspoons white wine vinegar

confectioners' sugar, for dusting

**For the frosting**

3 ounces white chocolate, coarsely chopped

1½ sticks unsalted butter, softened

3 cups confectioners' sugar

2 tablespoons milk

Preheat the oven to 350°F. Grease seven 2½-inch diameter baking rings, 1½ inches deep, line with parchment paper, and place on a baking sheet lined with parchment paper.

In a large bowl, beat together the eggs and sugar, using an electric handheld mixer, until pale. On slow speed, add the oil a little at a time until it has all been incorporated. Beat in the buttermilk, food coloring, and vanilla. Sift together the flour, cocoa powder, baking powder, and salt, then fold in, followed by the vinegar.

Divide the batter among the baking rings, filling them three-quarters full. Bake in the oven for 35 minutes, or until a toothpick inserted into the centers comes out clean.

Let cool in the rings for 5 minutes, then remove the cakes from the rings to a cooling rack to cool completely.

To make the frosting, melt the chocolate in a heatproof bowl set over a saucepan of barely simmering water, making sure the surface of the water does not touch the bowl. Let cool. Beat together the butter and half the confectioners' sugar until smooth, then add the remaining confectioners' sugar a little at a time, beating until the mixture is smooth. Add the milk and cooled chocolate and beat for another 2 minutes.

To assemble, slice a cake horizontally into three layers. Thinly spread a layer of frosting onto the bottom layer, then sandwich the middle layer on top. Spread a little more frosting on the middle layer, then add the top layer. Repeat with five of the mini cakes so that you have six cakes in total, with one extra cake without frosting. Spoon the remaining frosting into a pastry bag fitted with a plain piping tip, then pipe around the edges of the cakes until completely covered. Crumble the remaining unfrosted cake and sprinkle the crumbs over the tops of the piped cakes. Serve dusted with confectioners' sugar.

# Flour-free chocolate sponge

This is a great recipe, because the lack of flour makes this sponge really soft and moist and it is gluten free, too. It's so dark and chocolaty that I usually serve it with a little whipped cream and some fresh berries.

**Serves 6**

**Preparation time:** 10 minutes

**Cooking time:** 40 minutes

4 ounces semisweet chocolate, coarsely chopped

1 stick unsalted butter, softened, plus extra for greasing

¾ cup granulated sugar

3 eggs, beaten

1 teaspoon vanilla paste or extract

1 cup unsweetened cocoa powder

Preheat the oven to 325°F. Grease an 8-inch diameter, 2½-inch deep springform cake pan and line with parchment paper.

Melt the chocolate in a heatproof bowl set over a saucepan of barely simmering water, making sure the surface of the water does not touch the bowl. Let cool.

In a large bowl, cream together the butter and sugar, using an electric handheld mixer, until pale and fluffy. Beat in the eggs one at a time, followed by the cooled chocolate and the vanilla. Sift the cocoa powder and gently fold in.

Spoon the batter into the prepared pan and bake in the oven for 35 minutes, or until a toothpick inserted into the center comes out clean. Let cool in the pan for 10 minutes, then turn out onto a cooling rack.

## Tip

For an extra hit of cocoa, dust the inside of the greased pan with unsweetened cocoa powder.

# Soft cookie dough cookies

I simply adore these cookies. I love the soft centers, the rich flavor of the unrefined sugar, and all the additions of nuts, chocolate chips, or dried fruits, which make them so enticing and delicious.

**Makes 24**
**Preparation time:** 15 minutes
**Cooking time:** 25–30 minutes

1½ sticks unsalted butter, melted

1 cup firmly packed dark brown sugar

½ cup granulated sugar

1 teaspoon vanilla extract or paste

2 eggs

2 cups all-purpose flour

½ teaspoon baking soda

½ teaspoon salt

½ cup semisweet chocolate chips

½ cup white chocolate chips

1 cup coarsely chopped macadamia nuts

Preheat the oven to 350°F. Line two baking sheets with parchment paper.

In a large bowl, cream together the melted butter, brown sugar, and granulated sugar until smooth. Beat in the vanilla and eggs until light and creamy.

Sift together the flour, baking soda, and salt, then fold into the butter-and-sugar mixture until just combined. Stir in the chocolate chips and nuts.

Using an ice cream scoop, if possible, scoop the dough onto the prepared baking sheets, leaving at least 3½ inches between each cookie, because they will spread in the oven. Do not flatten them before baking.

Bake in the oven for 12–15 minutes, or until the edges look golden brown but the center is still soft. Let cool on the baking sheets for 5 minutes, then carefully transfer to a cooling rack to cool completely. Repeat with any remaining dough. Store the cookies in an airtight container for up to a few days.

## Tip

To vary the flavor, substitute the chocolate chips and macadamia nuts with dried fruits and different nuts.

# Dark chocolate moelleux

This extremely moist sponge is a perfect base for a celebration cake filled with a rich chocolate buttercream and coated with a glossy ganache. It looks great decorated with berries or dried fruits and nuts.

**Serves 12–14**

**Preparation time:** 30 minutes, plus cooling and setting

**Cooking time:** 40–45 minutes

2 ounces semisweet chocolate, coarsely chopped

3 sticks butter, softened, plus extra for greasing

1¾ cup granulated sugar

2½ tablespoons molasses

8 eggs, lightly beaten

2⅓ cups all-purpose flour

⅔ cup cocoa powder

1½ tablespoons baking powder

½ cup ground almonds (almond meal)

berries or dried fruits and nuts, to decorate

confectioners' sugar, for dusting

**For the ganache**

1 cup heavy cream

8 ounces semisweet chocolate, chopped

**For the buttercream**

1 ounce semisweet chocolate, coarsely chopped

1⅔ cups confectioners' sugar, sifted

1 stick unsalted butter, softened

a few drops of vanilla extract

2 tablespoons heavy cream

First, make the sponge. Preheat the oven to 325°F. Grease two 8½-inch diameter cake pans and line with parchment paper. Melt the chocolate in a heatproof bowl set over a saucepan of barely simmering water, making sure the surface of the water does not touch the bowl.

In a large bowl, cream together the butter and sugar until light and fluffy, then beat in the molasses. Beat in the eggs a little at a time, then add the melted chocolate. Sift together the flour, cocoa powder, and baking powder, then fold in with the ground almonds. Finish with an electric handheld mixer to produce a smooth, glossy consistency.

Divide the batter between the prepared pans and level the tops. Bake in the oven for 30–35 minutes, or until a toothpick inserted into the centers comes out clean. Let cool in the pans, then turn out onto a cooling rack.

To make the ganache, put the heavy cream into a saucepan and heat to just below boiling point. Remove from the heat and add the chocolate, then use a wooden spoon to beat vigorously until melted and smooth. Let cool to room temperature.

To make the buttercream, melt the chocolate as above and let cool. In a bowl, cream together the confectioners' sugar and butter, using an electric handheld mixer, until light and fluffy. Beat in the vanilla, cooled chocolate, and heavy cream to form a fairly stiff spreading consistency.

To assemble the cake, level the tops of the sponge cakes using a sharp knife. Spread the buttercream over the top of one of the cakes and place it on a cooling rack set over a large plate or baking sheet. Place the other cake, upside down, on top for a nice flat surface. Pour the ganache over the cake, completely covering it. Smooth with a spatula and let set at room temperature. Serve decorated with berries or dried fruits and nuts, and lightly dusted with confectioners' sugar.

# Chocolate gâteau Basque

This is a speciality from southwest France, just on the Spanish border. I've given this traditional gâteau a chocolate twist, which works wonders.

**Serves 8–10**

**Preparation time:** 30 minutes, plus chilling

**Cooking time:** 40–45 minutes

2 sticks unsalted butter, softened, plus extra for greasing

1 cup firmly packed light brown sugar

1¼ cups ground almonds (almond meal)

1 extra-large egg

1 teaspoon vanilla paste or extract

2⅓ cups all-purpose flour, plus extra for dusting

1 teaspoon baking powder

3 tablespoons unsweetened cocoa powder

1 egg yolk, beaten

**For the chocolate custard**

2 cups milk

½ cup light cream

¼ cup semolina

1 vanilla bean, split lengthwise

5 ounces semisweet chocolate, finely chopped

2 egg yolks

¾ cup superfine sugar or granulated sugar

3 tablespoons all-purpose flour

In a large bowl, beat together the butter, brown sugar, ground almonds, egg, and vanilla. Sift in the flour, baking powder, and cocoa powder, then combine together to form a dough without overkneading. Cover with plastic wrap and let rest in the refrigerator for at least 1 hour.

Meanwhile, make the custard. Put the milk, cream, semolina, and vanilla bean into a saucepan and bring to a boil. Remove the vanilla bean. Add the chocolate and stir until melted, then remove from the heat. Mix the 2 egg yolks with the superfine sugar in a bowl, then add the flour and beat until smooth. Pour a little of the hot chocolate milk onto the yolk mixture. Whisk well and pour back into the saucepan. Bring back to a boil and simmer for 2 minutes, whisking continuously. Transfer to a bowl and cover with plastic wrap. Let cool.

Preheat the oven to 350°F. Grease and flour an 8½-inch-diameter, 2-inch-deep round cake pan.

Roll out two-thirds of the dough on a floured surface and carefully use to line the pan. If the dough splits, gently mold it back together. Fill with the cold custard.

Roll out the remaining dough to a circle large enough to cover the top of the pan.

Brush the edge of the dough inside the pan with the beaten egg. Cover with the dough circle, then trim the edge and seal. Brush the top with more beaten egg and lightly mark the top in a crisscross design using a fork.

Place the pan on a wire rack over a baking sheet, then bake in the oven for 35–40 minutes, or until golden. Let cool completely before removing from the pan and serving.

# Chocolate and hazelnut muffins

Most muffin recipes come as a fruity option for breakfast. These rich muffins are more a mid-afternoon treat when served warm, straight from the oven.

**Makes 6**

**Preparation time:** 15 minutes

**Cooking time:** 25–30 minutes

3 ounces semisweet chocolate, coarsely chopped

¼ cup chocolate-and-hazelnut spread

1⅓ cups all-purpose flour

1 tablespoon baking powder

¼ cup unsweetened cocoa powder

¼ cup granulated sugar

2 eggs

1 teaspoon vanilla extract or paste

⅓ cup vegetable oil

¼ cup milk

½ cup dark chocolate chips

½ cup roasted and chopped hazelnuts (see Tip on page 44)

Preheat the oven to 350°F. Line a 6-cup muffin pan with paper muffin liners.

Gently melt the chocolate and chocolate spread in a heatproof bowl set over a saucepan of barely simmering water, making sure the surface of the water does not touch the bowl. Let cool for a few minutes.

Sift the flour, baking powder, and cocoa powder into a large bowl, then stir in the sugar. In a separate bowl, beat together the eggs, vanilla, oil, and milk using an electric handheld mixer. When combined, stir in the cooled chocolate. Fold the wet ingredients into the dry ingredients, using a rubber spatula or metal spoon, but don't overmix. Stir in the chocolate chips.

Divide the batter among the muffin liners, filling them three-quarters full, then sprinkle the hazelnuts over the tops. Bake in the oven for 20–25 minutes, or until a toothpick inserted into the centers comes out clean. When cooked, transfer to a cooling rack to cool.

## Tip

This recipe will make 12 small cakes if you use a shallow cupcake pan.

# Chocolate pain d'épice

Pain d'épice is a speciality from the east of France; this sticky loaf is usually served toasted with a spread of butter. This is my take on the traditional recipe, making it even more indulgent with chocolate.

**Serves 8**
**Preparation time:** 15 minutes, plus overnight chilling
**Cooking time:** 50–55 minutes

butter, for greasing

1 cup milk

½ cup honey

4 ounces semisweet chocolate, finely chopped

2½ cups whole-wheat flour

⅓ cup firmly packed light brown sugar

1 teaspoon baking soda

½ teaspoon ground cinnamon

½ teaspoon freshly grated nutmeg

½ teaspoon ground ginger

¼ teaspoon ground cloves

3 eggs, beaten

1 tablespoon vanilla extract or paste

1 tablespoon orange blossom water

Grease a 9 x 5 x 3-inch loaf pan and line with parchment paper.

Put the milk and honey into a small saucepan and heat gently but do not let it boil. Remove from the heat and add the chocolate, stirring until melted and blended together. Let cool for a few minutes.

Put the flour, sugar, baking soda, and spices into a large bowl and mix together. Make a well in the center, then stir in the eggs, vanilla, and orange blossom water, followed by the chocolate milk.

For best results, transfer the batter to a food processor and blend for 2–3 minutes or until smooth and glossy. Alternatively, mix well using a wooden spoon. Pour the batter into the prepared loaf pan, cover with plastic wrap, and let rest in the refrigerator overnight.

Preheat the oven to 350°F, and bake the loaf in the preheated oven for 45–50 minutes, or until a toothpick inserted into the center comes out clean. Let cool in the pan for 5 minutes, then transfer to a cooling rack to cool completely. The loaf keeps very well wrapped in plastic wrap in an airtight container for up to 2 weeks.

## Tip

Try toasting slices of this cake and spreading with butter or honey to serve.

# Double chocolate macaroons

Macaroons are still popular and fashionable, with more and more extraordinary flavors available. For me, you cannot beat a rich dark chocolate macaroon. I call these ones double, because they are sandwiched together with chocolate filling, too.

**Makes 28**

**Preparation time:** 30 minutes, plus standing and cooling

**Cooking time:** 25 minutes

1⅔ cups confectioners' sugar

1¼ cups ground almonds (almond meal)

3 tablespoons unsweetened cocoa powder

3 egg whites

2 tablespoons superfine sugar (or the same amount of granulated sugar processed in a food processor for 1 minute)

red paste food coloring

finely chopped semisweet chocolate, to decorate

**For the filling**

5 ounces semisweet chocolate, coarsely chopped

1 stick butter

3 tablespoons heavy cream

Start by making the filling. Melt the chocolate and butter with the cream in a heatproof bowl set over a saucepan of barely simmering water, making sure the surface of the water does not touch the bowl. Stir well until smooth, then let cool until thickened and a piping consistency but not hard.

Meanwhile, make the macaroons. Line four baking sheets with parchment paper. Put the confectioners' sugar, ground almonds, and cocoa powder into a food processor and grind to a fine powder. Sift the powder into a bowl.

In a separate, clean, dry bowl, whisk the egg whites to soft peaks, adding the superfine sugar a little at a time. Just before the whites are peaking, add a point of a knife of red food coloring (to enhance the natural reddish color of the cocoa powder). Using a rubber spatula, gradually fold the almond mixture into the egg whites until smooth and glossy but not runny.

Spoon the mixture into a pastry bag fitted with a plain piping tip, then pipe circles about 1¼ inches in diameter onto the prepared baking sheets. Let stand for 15 minutes at room temperature to let the tops start to dry. (In France, this is called *croutage*.) Meanwhile, preheat the oven to 300°F.

Bake in the oven for 20 minutes, or until the parchment paper peels off easily from the macaroons. Let cool completely on the baking sheets, then remove them from the parchment paper.

When the macaroons are cold, spoon the filling into a pastry bag, then pipe some ganache onto the bottom of a macaroon. Sandwich together with a second macaroon. Repeat with the remaining macaroons. Sprinkle with finely chopped semisweet chocolate to decorate before serving. Store the macaroons in airtight containers for up to a few days. It is best not to put them in the refrigerator, because this makes them sticky.

# Salted butter caramel cake

I am a huge fan of salted butter caramel, and after plenty of experiments, I've come up with this delicious recipe, which is made of layers of salted butter caramel cookie baked into a rich and dark chocolate cake, a winning recipe.

**Serves 8–10**

**Preparation time:** 35 minutes, plus chilling and cooling

**Cooking time:** 45 minutes

8 ounces semisweet chocolate, coarsely chopped

1 stick unsalted butter, plus extra for greasing

150ml (¼ pint) milk

4 eggs, separated

⅔ cup granulated sugar

¾ cup all-purpose flour

pinch of sea salt crystals, to decorate

**For the caramel cookie**

8 ounces graham crackers (about 2 cups when crumbs)

1½ cups granulated sugar

2 tablespoons water

½ cup light cream

1 stick salted butter, plus extra for greasing

2 pinches of sea salt

**For the chocolate glaze**

8 ounces semiswseet chocolate, chopped

1 cup light cream

First, make the caramel cookie. Grease two 8½-inch diameter cake pans and line the bottoms with parchment paper.

Put the graham crackers into a food processor and process to fine crumbs. Put the sugar and water into a heavy saucepan and dissolve over low heat. Increase the heat and cook until it forms an amber caramel. Remove from the heat and carefully stir in the cream, followed by the butter and salt. Stir the cookie crumbs into the caramel, then divide equally between the prepared pans and press down with the back of a spoon. Place in the freezer to set.

To make the sponge cake, preheat the oven to 350°F. Grease a deep 8½-inch diameter loose-bottom cake pan and line with parchment paper.

Melt the chocolate and butter with the milk in a heatproof bowl set over a saucepan of barely simmering water, making sure the surface of the water does not touch the bowl.

In a large bowl, beat together the egg yolks and sugar, using an electric handheld mixer, until pale and fluffy. Stir in the chocolate mixture, then fold in the flour. In a clean, dry bowl, whisk the egg whites to soft peaks, then gently fold into the chocolate mixture.

Remove the caramel cookie circles from the freezer and remove them from the pans, discarding the lining paper. Place one of the circles on the bottom of the prepared loose-bottom cake tin and spread with half of the cake batter. Lay the other cookie circle on top and cover with the remaining cake batter.

Bake in the oven for 25–30 minutes, until the cake is just cooked—it should be almost undercooked for extra gooeyness. Let cool in the pan for 10 minutes, then turn out onto a cooling rack to cool completely.

To make the glaze, put the chocolate into a heatproof bowl. Put the cream into a saucepan and heat to simmering point, then pour one-quarter over the chocolate. Let rest for 1 minute, until the chocolate starts to melt, then gently stir in the rest of the cream until smooth and glossy.

Cover the cooled cake with the chocolate glaze and use a spatula to spread it evenly over the top and down the side. Lightly sprinkle sea salt crystals on top of the cake, then chill it in the refrigerator until set before serving.

# Swiss walnut and chocolate cake

I used to make this recipe when I was a kid. I'm not too sure where the Swiss origin comes from, but even today it is still one of my all-time favorite cakes to make, because I love the combination of walnuts and chocolate.

**Serves 8**

**Preparation time:** 15 minutes, plus cooling

**Cooking time:** 40–45 minutes

4 ounces semisweet chocolate, coarsely chopped

1¼ sticks unsalted butter, softened, plus extra for greasing

¾ cup granulated sugar

2 eggs

⅔ cup all-purpose flour

2 teaspoons baking powder

2 teaspoons vanilla paste or extract

½ cup roasted and chopped walnuts (see Tip below)

confectioners' sugar, for dusting

½ cup walnut halves, to decorate

Preheat the oven to 350°F. Grease an 8½-inch diameter cake pan and line with parchment paper.

Melt the chocolate in a heatproof bowl set over a saucepan of barely simmering water, making sure the surface of the water does not touch the bowl. Let cool for a few minutes.

In a large bowl, cream together the butter and sugar until pale and fluffy. Beat in the eggs one at the time. Sift together the flour and baking powder, then carefully fold in. Add the cooled chocolate and the vanilla, then fold in the chopped walnuts.

Spoon the batter into the prepared pan. Arrange the extra walnut halves on top in a circular pattern and bake in the oven for 30–35 minutes, or until a toothpick inserted into the center comes out clean—the texture will be similar to a brownie.

Let cool in the pan for 10 minutes, then remove from the pan and transfer to a cooling rack. Serve dusted with confectioners' sugar. A hot crème anglaise (a thin custard) or freshly whipped cream, is perfect as an accompaniment

## Tip

For roasted walnuts or any other nuts, simply spread whole nuts over a baking sheet and roast in the oven at 350°F for 8–10 minutes, or until golden and crisp—be sure to watch them, because they can burn quickly. Let cool, then chop.

# White chocolate and peach melba muffins

Theses muffins are the perfect summer Sunday brunch because they are so delightfully fruity, fresh, and delicious. My favorite and hopefully yours once tasted …

**Makes 12**
**Preparation time:** 15 minutes
**Cooking time:** 25 minutes

2⅓ cups all-purpose flour

2 teaspoons baking powder

1 egg

¾ cup granulated sugar

1 teaspoon vanilla extract or paste

1 cup milk

4 tablespoons unsalted butter, melted and cooled

1 small peach, skinned, pitted, and chopped, or ¾ cup chopped canned peaches

4 ounces white chocolate, cut into small chunks

¾ cup fresh raspberries

confectioners' sugar, for dusting

Preheat the oven to 350°F. Line a 12-cup muffin pan with paper muffin liners.

Sift the flour and baking powder into a bowl. In a separate bowl, beat together the egg and sugar, using an electric handheld mixer, then beat in the vanilla, milk, and cooled melted butter. Using a rubber spatula or metal spoon, fold the wet ingredients into the dry ingredients until the mixture is smooth, but don't overmix. Briefly fold in the peaches and white chocolate.

Divide the batter among the muffin liners, filling them three-quarters full. Bake in the oven for 25 minutes, or until a toothpick inserted into the centers comes out clean. Let cool on a cooling rack.

In a small bowl, roughly crush the raspberries with a fork. Spoon them on top of the muffins just before serving. Decorate with a dusting of confectioners' sugar.

# Chocolate and pistachio biscotti

Originally from Italy, biscotti now adorn coffee shops across the world—they are the perfect combination with good coffee. These chocolate and pistachio ones are to die for.

**Makes 26**

**Preparation time:** 20 minutes, plus cooling

**Cooking time:** 50–55 minutes

1 stick unsalted butter, softened, plus extra for greasing

1 cup granulated sugar

2 eggs

2¼ cups all-purpose flour, plus extra for dusting

⅔ cup unsweetened cocoa powder

1 teaspoon baking soda

1 cup shelled pistachio nuts

½ cup semisweet chocolate chips

Preheat the oven to 350°F. Lightly grease two large baking sheets.

In a large bowl, cream together the butter and sugar until pale and fluffy. Beat in the eggs one at a time, then sift together the flour, cocoa powder, and baking soda and fold in. Gently stir in the pistachios and chocolate chips.

Turn out the batter onto a floured surface and form into a large, slightly flattened loaf shape, about 12 x 3 inches. Carefully transfer to one of the prepared baking sheets and bake for 30 minutes. Remove from the oven and let cool for 10 minutes. Reduce the oven temperature to 300°F.

Place the warm loaf on a cutting board and slice into ½-inch-thick slices. Arrange them on the baking sheets and return to the oven for another 20–25 minutes, or until dry and crispy. Once cooked, transfer to a cooling rack to cool and harden.

You can store the biscotti in airtight containers for up to 2 weeks. They also make really nice presents when wrapped in a gift bag.

# Chocolate florentines

These little treats are great as a gift when boxed or bagged beautifully and they make a great accompaniment for after-dinner coffee.

**Makes 8**

**Preparation time:** 20 minutes, plus cooling and setting

**Cooking time:** 8 minutes

4 tablespoons unsalted butter, softened, plus extra for greasing

¼ cup firmly packed light brown sugar

2 tablespoons all-purpose flour

¼ slivered almonds, toasted

¼ cup roasted and chopped hazelnuts (see Tip on page 44)

¼ cup roasted and chopped walnuts (see Tip on page 44)

¼ cup candied peel

5 ounces milk chocolate, coarsely chopped

Preheat the oven to 350°F. Grease a baking sheet or 4-inch silicone florentine molds.

In a bowl, cream together the butter and sugar until pale and fluffy. Sift in the flour, then fold in all the nuts and the peel.

Place eight heaping spoonfuls of the dough on the prepared baking sheet, leaving enough space between each to expand, or fill the molds. Bake in the oven for 6–7 minutes, or until the florentines are golden. Let cool on the baking sheet or in the molds until cold.

Melt the chocolate in a heatproof bowl set over a saucepan of barely simmering water, making sure the surface of the water does not touch the bowl. Using a pastry brush, coat the bottom of each florentine with the melted chocolate. Before the chocolate sets, create waves in the chocolate using a fork, then place, chocolate side up, on parchment paper to set at room temperature. Store in a cool, dry place for up to 2 weeks.

## Tip

To vary the flavors, replace the nuts with shelled pistachios, pine nuts, or candied cherries.

# Chocolate rum and raisin loaf

I usually keep the combination of rum and raisin for ice cream, but I will always make an exception for this very tasty loaf, because it is really the perfect combination and texture.

**Serves 8**
**Preparation time:** 25 minutes, plus soaking overnight and cooling
**Cooking time:** 50 minutes

1 stick unsalted butter, plus extra for greasing

5 ounces semisweet chocolate, coarsely chopped

4 eggs, separated

1 cup granulated sugar

½ cup ground almonds (almond meal)

¾ cup all-purpose flour

1 tablespoon baking powder

**For the rum and raisin ganache**

½ cup raisins

3 tablespoons dark rum

¾ cup light cream

2 tablespoons granulated sugar

12 ounces semisweet chocolate, chopped

2 tablespoons unsalted butter, softened

For the rum and raisin ganache, put the raisins and rum into a small bowl and let soak overnight.

Preheat the oven to 350°F. Grease a 9 x 5 x 3-inch loaf pan and line with parchment paper.

To make the cake, melt the butter and chocolate in a heatproof bowl set over a saucepan of barely simmering water, making sure the surface of the water does not touch the bowl. Let cool for a few minutes.

In a large bowl, beat together the egg yolks and sugar, using an electric handheld mixer, until pale and creamy. Add the cooled chocolate mixture with the ground almonds. Sift together the flour and baking powder, then beat in. In a large, clean, dry bowl, whisk the egg whites to stiff peaks, then gently fold into the mixture.

Spoon the batter into the prepared pan and bake in the oven for 45 minutes, or until a toothpick inserted into the center comes out clean. Let cool in the pan for 5–10 minutes, then turn out onto a cooling rack to cool completely.

To make the rum and raisin ganache, put the cream and sugar into a saucepan and heat until steaming hot, but do not let it boil. Remove from the heat and add the chocolate, stirring until smooth and glossy. Gently stir in the butter, then fold in the soaked raisins.

To glaze the cake, place the cake on a cooling rack set over a large plate or baking sheet. Spread the warm ganache all over the cake and smooth it evenly using a spatula. Lift carefully onto a serving plate before the ganache sets. I like to sprinkle shredded gold leaf over the glossy cake for a touch of glamour!

# Chocolate financiers with citrus crumb topping

Financiers have been around for hundreds of years. These soft, classic petits fours are mostly made of ground nuts, such as almonds or hazelnuts—the addition of chocolate and the zesty topping make this version really special.

**Makes 24**

**Preparation time:** 20 minutes

**Cooking time:** 12–15 minutes

1½ ounces semisweet chocolate, coarsely chopped

6 tablespoons unsalted butter, softened, plus extra for greasing

½ cup ground almonds (almond meal)

⅔ cup confectioners' sugar

⅓ cup all-purpose flour

4 egg whites

grated lemon zest, to decorate

**For the citrus crumb topping**

2 tablespoons unsalted butter

finely grated zest of 1 lemon

2 drops of lemon extract

3 tablespoons all-purpose flour

2 tablespoons confectioners' sugar

½ cup ground almonds (almond meal)

Preheat the oven to 350°F. Lightly grease two 12-cup silicone financier molds or cupcake pans.

First make the citrus crumb topping. Put the butter into a bowl and mix in the lemon zest and extract. Add all the remaining ingredients and rub, in using your fingertips, until the mixture resembles fine bread crumbs. Put to one side.

Melt the chocolate and butter in a heatproof bowl set over a saucepan of barely simmering water, making sure the surface of the water does not touch the bowl. Let cool for a few minutes.

Mix the ground almonds, confectioners' sugar, and flour into the cooled chocolate mixture. In a large, clean, dry bowl, whisk the egg whites to soft peaks, then gently fold into the chocolate mixture.

Divide the batter between the cups of the pans, filling them three-quarters full. Generously sprinkle the citrus crumb topping over the batter and bake in the oven for 10–12 minutes. Let cool in the pans for 5 minutes, then transfer to a cooling rack. Sprinkle with grated lemon zest to decorate before serving.

If you manage not to eat them all immediately, any remaining financiers will freeze well.

# Chocolate waffles

As kids, we used to love going to Belgium for two reasons—first, the light, fluffy waffle, and second, the famous chocolate. This is my homage to these great trips—a combination of both waffle and chocolate.

**Makes 12–16**

**Preparation time:** 5 minutes

**Cooking time:** 5 minutes per waffle

⅔ cup unsweetened cocoa powder

2 teaspoon ground cinnamon

2 sticks butter, melted

1½ cups granulated sugar

4 eggs, beaten

2 cups all-purpose flour

2 tablespoons milk

2 teaspoons vanilla paste or extract

confectioners' sugar and
unsweetened cocoa powder,
for dusting

Preheat a waffle iron. Sift the cocoa powder into a large bowl and stir in the cinnamon and melted butter. Add the sugar, eggs, and flour, then whisk in the milk and vanilla until smooth.

Fill the waffle iron with some of the batter and cook according to the manufacturer's instructions. Repeat until all the batter is used.

Dust the waffles with confectioners' sugar and cocoa powder and serve warm. These are great served with one of the chocolate sauces on pages 168–69.

# Breton shortbread with chocolate

Every pâtisserie or bakery in my birth region of Brittany will have this speciality in their display … and each one will keep its recipe a secret! Here, I am sharing my grandmother Camille's recipe.

**Serves 8**
**Preparation time:** 15 minutes
**Cooking time:** 40–45 minutes

2¾ cups all-purpose flour

1¼ cups granulated sugar

2 sticks salted butter, cubed, plus extra for greasing

6 egg yolks

2 tablespoons dark rum

2 teaspoons vanilla extract

1 cup semisweet chocolate chips

Preheat the oven to 350°F. Grease a 9½-inch diameter tart pan and line the bottom with parchment paper.

Put the flour and sugar into a bowl and mix together. Add the butter and rub in, using your fingertips, until the mixture resembles fine bread crumbs. In a separate bowl, beat five of the egg yolks with the rum and vanilla extract, then mix into the dry ingredients. Stir in the chocolate chips.

Spread the batter into the prepared pan. Beat the remaining egg yolk, then brush over the top. Using a fork, make a crisscross design across the top.

Bake in the oven for 40–45 minutes, or until golden and cooked through. Let cool in the pan for a few minutes, then carefully turn out onto a cooling rack to cool completely.

# Chocolate shortbreads

For more than ten years, I was a member of the beautiful Skibo Castle in Scotland. These chocolate shortbreads were always one of the highlights of the trip to this retreat.

**Makes 18**
**Preparation time:** 15 minutes, plus chilling
**Cooking time:** 10–12 minutes

1¼ sticks salted butter, softened, plus extra for greasing
½ cup firmly packed light brown sugar
2 teaspoons vanilla paste or extract
1⅓ cups all-purpose flour
scant ⅓ cup unsweetened cocoa powder
1 cup semisweet chocolate chips
⅓ cup superfine sugar or granulated sugar

In a large bowl, cream together the butter, brown sugar, and vanilla until pale and fluffy. Sift together the flour and cocoa powder, fold in, and combine to form a crumbly dough. Stir in the chocolate chips.

Sprinkle the superfine sugar onto a clean work surface. Form the dough into a 2-inch diameter log, then roll in the sugar to coat. Cover with plastic wrap and let rest in the refrigerator for at least 2 hours.

Preheat the oven to 350°F and grease two large baking sheets.

Using a large knife, cut the dough into ½-inch-thick circles and place on the prepared baking sheets. Bake in the oven for 10–12 minutes, or until the edges are firm to the touch. Let cool on the sheets, then store in an airtight container or cookie jar for up to 1 week.

# Crispy malted chocolate meringues

I've always been a huge fan of meringues, but they need to dry out properly to achieve a lovely crunch and a chewy center. The addition of the malt powder and the sexy swirls of chocolate make these superspecial.

**Makes 6**

**Preparation time:** 15 minutes, plus cooling

**Cooking time:** 2 hours 5 minutes

5 ounces semisweet chocolate, coarsely chopped

3 egg whites

½ cup superfine sugar (or the same amount of granulated sugar processed in a food processor for 1 minute)

¾ cup confectioners' sugar

¼ cup unsweetened cocoa powder

2 tablespoons malt powder (malt flour)

Preheat the oven to 225°F. Line two baking sheets with parchment paper.

Melt the chocolate in a heatproof bowl set over a saucepan of barely simmering water, making sure the surface of the water does not touch the bowl.

In a clean, dry bowl, beat the egg whites, using an electric handheld mixer, to soft peaks. Add the superfine sugar a little at a time, beating continuously until the mixture is glossy. Sift together the confectioners' sugar, cocoa powder, and malt powder, then fold into the egg whites using a rubber spatula. Gently swirl the melted chocolate into the meringue mixture to form a marbled effect.

Spoon the meringue into six large dollops on the prepared baking sheets (I like mine to be slightly misshapen) and place in the oven for 2 hours, then turn the oven off and let the meringues rest inside to cool completely.

When cold, remove from the parchment paper and store in airtight containers for up to 1 week. I like to serve these meringues piled high with unsweetened whipped cream and a generous dusting of grated semisweet chocolate.

## Tip

Always use a clean, dry bowl to whisk or beat egg whites, because any trace of grease will prevent perfect peaks from forming.

# Chocolate Kouglof

Alsace and the east of France are famous for their baking and cooking. The Kouglof is a traditional recipe baked in a mold with a characteristic shape. As well as looking good it tastes divine.

**Serves 8–10**

**Preparation time:** 35 minutes, plus soaking and chilling overnight, and rising and cooling

**Cooking time:** 50–55 minutes

½ cup golden raisins

½ cup Cognac

2 tablespoons plus ¾ teaspoon active dry yeast

½ cup granulated sugar

½ cup lukewarm milk

4 cups all-purpose flour, plus extra for dusting

2 pinches of salt

3 eggs

1¾ sticks unsalted butter, cubed, plus extra for greasing

½ cup chopped almonds

2 tablespoons candied peel

½ cup semisweet chocolate chips

**For the glaze**

5 ounces semisweet chocolate, coarsely chopped

4 tablespoons unsalted butter

2 tablespoons confectioners' sugar

Put the golden raisins and brandy into a bowl and let soak overnight at room temperature.

The following day, put the yeast, sugar, and milk in a separate bowl and mix gently to dissolve. Let stand for 10 minutes.

Sift the flour and salt into the bowl of a freestanding mixer fitted with a dough hook. Add the eggs and yeast mixture and mix together for 10 minutes, or until the dough comes away from the side of the bowl. Add the butter a little at a time until well incorporated. Add the remaining ingredients, including the soaked raisins, and mix for another 5 minutes.

Grease and flour a 2-quart kouglof mold. Push the dough into it, cover with plastic wrap, and chill in the refrigerator overnight. The following day, remove the mold from the refrigerator and let the dough rise for 4–5 hours at room temperature.

Preheat the oven to 325°F and bake the kouglof in the preheated oven for 45–50 minutes, or until golden. Turn out of the mold onto a cooling rack and let cool completely.

To make the glaze, melt the chocolate and butter in a heatproof bowl set over a saucepan of barely simmering water, making sure the surface of the water does not touch the bowl. When melted, fold in the sugar. Pour the glaze over the top of the cake and let set. Traditionally, this cake is served with beaten crème fraîche, but you can serve it with freshly whipped cream.

# Chocolate, squash, and pecan cake

I'd describe this cake as a perfect winter warmer, full of very earthy flavors and a spicy, nutty crunch. It's best eaten a day after baking.

**Serves 8**

**Preparation time:** 20 minutes, plus cooling and resting overnight

**Cooking time:** 1 hour 25 minutes

1 cup pecans

1 teaspoon cayenne pepper

8 ounces semisweet chocolate, coarsely chopped

1¼ sticks unsalted butter, plus extra for greasing 3 eggs

1¼ cups firmly packed dark brown sugar

1 cup plus 2 tablespoons water

3 teaspoon vanilla paste or extract

2 cups all-purpose flour

2 teaspoons baking powder

1 tablespoon ground cinnamon

1¼ cups, peeled, seeded, and shredded butternut squash

unsweetened cocoa powder, for dusting

Preheat the oven to 325°F. Grease a 9-inch diameter springform cake pan and line with parchment paper.

In a large bowl, mix together the pecans and cayenne pepper. Place the nuts on a baking sheet and roast in the oven for 10 minutes, or until they are golden and crunchy. Let cool, then coarsely chop.

Melt the chocolate and butter in a heatproof bowl set over a saucepan of barely simmering water, making sure the surface of the water does not touch the bowl.

Beat together the eggs and sugar in a bowl until nice and smooth, then beat in the melted chocolate mixture, followed by the water and vanilla. Sift together the flour, baking powder, and cinnamon, then fold in until smooth. Fold in the pumpkin and chopped pecans.

Spoon the batter into the prepared pan and bake in the oven for 1 hour 10 minutes, or until a toothpick inserted into the center comes out clean. Let cool in the pan for 10 minutes, then turn out onto a cooling rack to cool completely.

Wrap the cake in plastic wrap and store at room temperature for at least 24 hours before eating. Dust with cocoa powder before serving.

Apricot and chocolate charlotte

Desserts

# Apricot and chocolate charlotte

This was my mom's favorite recipe. She used to make this spectacular dessert on Sunday when we had guests. It has to be made the day before, which makes your life easier on the day if you are entertaining.

**Serves 6**
**Preparation time:** 30 minutes, plus cooling and chilling overnight
**Cooking time:** 15 minutes

butter, for greasing
30–35 ladyfinger cookies

**For the apricots**
¼ water
½o cup granulated sugar
6–7 fresh apricots (about 10 ounces), pitted and diced
juice of 1 lemon
½ tablespoon unsalted butter
2 teaspoons honey
1 tablespoon apricot preserves
2 teaspoons balsamic vinegar

**For the chocolate mousse**
4 ounces semisweet chocolate, coarsely chopped
2 tablespoons unsalted butter
3 tablespoons crème fraîche
2 egg yolks
3½ egg whites (7 tablespoons)
1 tablespoon superfine sugar or granulated sugar

Start with the apricots. Put the water and sugar into a saucepan and heat gently until the sugar has dissolved. Put the apricots into a heatproof bowl, then pour the syrup over them and add the lemon juice. Let cool, then drain the apricots, reserving the syrup.

Melt the butter in a small skillet. Add the apricots and sauté until golden. Remove from the heat and add the honey, apricot preserves, and vinegar. Return to the heat and cook for another 2 minutes, then let cool.

For the chocolate mousse, melt the chocolate and butter in a heatproof bowl set over a saucepan of barely simmering water, making sure the surface of the water does not touch the bowl. Remove from the heat and fold in the crème fraîche, then the egg yolks. In a clean, dry bowl, whisk the egg whites and sugar to stiff peaks, then gently fold into the chocolate mixture to form a smooth mousse.

To make the charlotte, lightly grease a 6-inch diameter charlotte mold and line the bottom with parchment paper. Dip the ladyfingers into the reserved apricot syrup, then use to carefully line the charlotte mold, making sure they are tightly placed.

Spoon one-third of the chocolate mousse over the bottom, spoon over half of the cooled apricots, then cover with a layer of dipped ladyfingers. Repeat the layers, finishing with a layer of ladyfingers. If necessary, trim off any excess ladyfingers from around the edge to level the top. Cover the top with wax paper and place a few small plates on top as weights. Let chill in the refrigerator overnight.

One hour before serving, turn the charlotte out onto a serving plate and let stand at room temperature. Decorate with any leftover apricots and serve with crème fraîche or freshly whipped cream. See previous page for finished result.

**1.** Sauté the apricots in honey, apricot preserves, and balsamic vinegar.

**2.** Whisk the egg whites, then fold them into the melted chocolate mixture.

**3.** Grease and line the bottom of a charlotte mold, then line with ladyfingers.

**4.** Spoon some chocolate mixture into the bottom, then add half of the apricots.

**5.** Add a layer of ladyfingers dipped in the apricot syrup.

**6.** Repeat the chocolate and apricot layers, finishing with a layer of ladyfingers. Cover, then weigh down the top and chill in the refrigerator before turning out.

# Chocolate petits pots

If you like a small treat at the end of a meal, this recipe is for you.
It's a classic you will find in most French bistros, and because of its
size, it won't make you feel too guilty.

**Serves 8**

**Preparation time:** 10 minutes,
plus cooling and chilling

**Cooking time:** 5 minutes

4 cups milk

8 ounces semisweet chocolate,
coarsely chopped

¼ cup firmly packed light
brown sugar

⅔ cup cornstarch

4 tablespoons unsalted butter,
cut into small cubes

2 teaspoon brandy

Reserve ⅔ cup of the milk and pour the remainder
into a small saucepan. Add the semisweet chocolate
and sugar and heat gently, stirring until the sugar
has completely dissolved.

Blend the cornstarch with the reserved milk in a bowl
using a small wire whisk, then stir into the chocolate
milk and bring to a boil, stirring continuously. Remove
from the heat and add the butter, then stir in the brandy.

Pour into eight small cups or ramekin dishes. Let cool,
then let set in the refrigerator for at least 4 hours.
Remove from the refrigerator 1 hour before serving.

# Tip

To vary the flavor, substitute the brandy with orange
liqueur, kirsch, cassis, or framboise.

# Gâteau Concorde

This recipe was created by the godfather of modern pâtisserie,
Gaston Lenôtre. If you like chocolate and meringue, this is cake heaven!

**Serves 8**

**Preparation time:** 40 minutes,
plus cooling and chilling

**Cooking time:** 1 hour 35 minutes

4 ounces semisweet chocolate,
coarsely chopped

6 tablespoons unsalted butter

3 egg yolks

5 egg whites

confectioners' sugar and
unsweetened cocoa powder,
for dusting

**For the meringues**

5 egg whites

¾ cup superfine sugar (or the
same quantity of granulated sugar
processed in the food processor for
1 minute)

1¼ cups confectioners' sugar

⅓ cup plus 1 tablespoon
unsweetened cocoa powder

First make the meringues. Preheat the oven to 300°F. Line four baking
sheets with parchment paper, then draw an 8½-inch diameter circle on
three of the papers.

In a large, clean, dry bowl, whisk the egg whites to stiff peaks, adding
the superfine sugar a little at a time. Sift together the confectioners' sugar
and cocoa powder, then gently fold into the meringue mixture.

Spoon the mixture into a pastry bag fitted with a ½-inch diameter plain
piping tip, then pipe the mixture onto the three marked circles on the
parchment paper. Using the remaining mixture, pipe long, thin lengths
of meringue on the remaining baking sheet. Bake all the meringues in
the oven for 1 hour 30 minutes, until crisp. Remove from the oven and
let cool.

Next, make a chocolate mousse. Melt the chocolate in a heatproof bowl
set over a saucepan of barely simmering water, making sure the surface
of the water does not touch the bowl. Remove from the heat and stir in
the butter, then the egg yolks. In a large, clean, dry bowl, whisk the egg
whites to soft peaks, then gently fold in the chocolate mixture. Cover
and chill in the refrigerator for a few minutes until set enough to pipe.

To assemble the cake, spoon just over half of the chocolate mousse into
a pastry bag fitted with a ½-inch diameter plain piping tip, then pipe a
little of the mousse onto a serving plate to secure one of the meringue
circles on top. Pipe the mousse all over the meringue, then place another
circle on top, gently pressing down to secure. Pipe another layer of mousse
on top, then place the remaining circle, upside down, on top to create a
flat surface. Using a spatula, spread the remaining mousse over the top
and sides.

Cut the lengths of meringue into ¾-inch pieces with a sharp knife, then
randomly place over the cake until it is completely covered. Cover with
plastic wrap and chill in the refrigerator for at least 4 hours. To serve,
dust with confectioners' sugar, then a slight dusting of cocoa powder.

# Tip

Make the meringues the day before serving so that they are really dry.

# Chocolate and tonka bean crème brûlées

Tonka beans are sweet and deliciously perfumed with vanilla and rich milk chocolate. This strong spice adds a touch of suave luxury to the brûlées.

**Serves 6**

**Preparation time:** 15 minutes, plus chilling overnight

**Cooking time:** 1 hour 10 minutes

4 ounces semisweet chocolate, finely chopped

1 tonka bean

2½ cups heavy cream

8 egg yolks

⅓ cup granulated sugar

¼ cup demerara sugar or other raw sugar

Preheat the oven to 225°F. Place six brûlée dishes or flameproof ramekins into a shallow roasting pan and fill the pan with water to come halfway up the sides of the dishes.

Put the chocolate into a heatproof bowl. Using a nutmeg grater, grate the tonka bean, then mix with the chocolate. Put the cream into a saucepan and heat to just below boiling point, then pour over the chocolate and mix gently until the chocolate has melted.

In a separate bowl, beat together the egg yolks and granulated sugar using an electric handheld mixer until pale and fluffy. Beat the chocolate cream, a little at a time, into the egg mixture.

Pour into the dishes in the bain-marie and bake in the oven for 1 hour, or until set.

Let cool, then chill in the refrigerator overnight.

To serve, sprinkle demerara sugar over the top of each crème, then caramelize using a kitchen blowtorch.

## Tip

If you do not have a kitchen blowtorch, sprinkle the crème brûlées with the sugar and put on a baking sheet. Place under a hot broiler until the sugar caramelizes.

# Raspberry and chocolate tart

As well as the great combination of semisweet chocolate and raspberries, the addition of the chocolate pastry provides a three-dimensional taste and texture to this yummy recipe.

**Serves 6**

**Preparation time:** 25 minutes, plus chilling and cooling

**Cooking time:** 25 minutes

1⅓ cups all-purpose flour, plus extra for dusting

⅔ cup unsweetened cocoa powder

⅓ cup confectioners' sugar

1¼ sticks unsalted butter, cubed, plus extra for greasing

3 egg yolks

1 teaspoon vanilla extract

4 cups raspberries (about 1 pound)

confectioners' sugar, for dusting

**For the ganache**

8 ounces semisweet chocolate, coarsely chopped

1 cup light cream

2 teaspoons vanilla extract

6 tablespoons unsalted butter

Sift together the flour, cocoa powder, and confectioners' sugar into a large bowl. Add the butter and rub in using your fingertips until the mixture resembles fine bread crumbs. Add the egg yolks and gently mix together, then add the vanilla and combine to form a smooth dough. Cover with plastic wrap and let rest in the refrigerator for at least 30 minutes.

Preheat the oven to 375°F. Lightly grease a 9½-inch diameter tart pan.

Roll out the dough on a lightly floured surface and carefully use to line the pan. Cover with parchment paper, fill the pastry shell with pie weights or dried beans, and bake in the oven for 15 minutes. Remove the paper and weights and return to the oven for another 5 minutes. Let cool.

To make the ganache, melt the chocolate in a heatproof bowl set over a saucepan of barely simmering water, making sure the surface of the water does not touch the bowl. Meanwhile, put the cream into a saucepan and heat until steaming hot, but do not let it boil. Remove the melted chocolate from the heat and slowly pour in the cream, gently stirring the mixture. Add the vanilla, then the butter, and stir together.

Pack the cooled pastry shell with raspberries, saving a few for decoration. Pour the hot chocolate ganache over the raspberries to fill to the top of the pastry. Let set in the refrigerator for at least 30 minutes. Serve decorated with the reserved raspberries dusted with a little confectioners' sugar.

# Pear and chocolate clafoutis

Clafoutis is a rustic dish usually made with cherries. This dessert has had a little revival and you will love this combination. I make it with raw pears to give a nice crunch.

**Serves 6**

**Preparation time:** 20 minutes, plus chilling

**Cooking time:** 25–30 minutes

unsalted butter, for greasing

1 tablespoon packed light brown sugar

8 ounces semisweet chocolate, coarsely chopped

⅓ cup all-purpose flour

1 teaspoon ground cinnamon

4 eggs

¼ cup heavy cream

1 cup milk

4 ripe pears, peeled, cored, and thickly sliced

Preheat the oven to 350°F. Grease a 1½-quart shallow, ceramic baking dish and sprinkle with the sugar.

Melt the chocolate in a heatproof bowl set over a saucepan of barely simmering water, making sure the surface of the water does not touch the bowl.

Sift together the flour and cinnamon into a bowl, then beat in the eggs, cream, and milk to form a batter. Stir in the melted chocolate, then pour it into the prepared dish. Sprinkle the pears all over the chocolate custard, letting them sink.

Bake in the oven for 20–25 minutes, or until set. Let cool completely in the dish, then chill in the refrigerator before serving.

# Chocolate and blackberry mille feuille

You can't beat the lightness, flakiness, and buttery texture of a good mille feuille. The combination of the cassis and blackberries makes this version very sophisticated.

**Serves 8**

**Preparation time:** 30 minutes, plus cooling

**Cooking time:** 20–30 minutes

1 (1-pound) package ready-to-bake all-butter puff pastry

all-purpose flour, for dusting

¼ cup unsweetened cocoa powder

2¾ cups blackberries

confectioners' sugar and unsweetened cocoa powder, for dusting

**For the chocolate cream**

4 ounces semisweet chocolate, chopped

½ cup light cream

2 cups heavy cream

2 tablespoons crème de cassis, plus extra for drizzling

Preheat the oven to 425°F. Roll out the pastry on a lightly floured surface to a large rectangle and sift half of the cocoa powder over it. Fold one end of the rectangle into the center and repeat with the opposite end, so that each end meets in the middle. Repeat the process, adding another dusting of cocoa powder, then roll out the pastry to a thin rectangle, about 13½ x 11 inches.

Place the pastry on a large baking sheet and trim to fit if necessary. Prick the pastry all over with a fork, cover with a sheet of parchment paper, and weigh the pastry down with a second baking sheet.

Bake in the oven for 10–15 minutes, or until the pastry begins to brown. Remove the top baking sheet and parchment paper, then return to the oven for another 5–10 minutes, or until cooked. Let cool.

Meanwhile, make the chocolate cream. Put the chocolate into a large heatproof bowl. Put the light cream into a saucepan and heat to just below boiling point. Pour the cream onto the chocolate, stirring gently until smooth. Let cool. Whip the heavy cream to soft peaks. Mix the cooled chocolate mixture into the whipped cream, then fold in the crème de cassis.

To assemble, cut the cooled pastry into 16 small rectangles. Using a pastry bag or spatula, pipe or spread a thick layer of the chocolate cream onto all the pastry rectangles. Arrange the blackberries on half of the rectangles, reserving eight for decoration, then add a little more chocolate cream between the berries. Sandwich the cream-covered pastry rectangles on top of the berries and dust with confectioners' sugar and cocoa powder.

Cut the reserved berries in half, drizzle with cassis, and use to decorate the mille feuille.

# Gâteau opéra

This is another great French classic that you will find in pâtisserie windows all over France. It's also one of the best sellers at my London cake boutique.

**Serves 8**

**Preparation time:** 1 hour, plus cooling and chilling

**Cooking time:** 25 minutes

3 egg whites

1 tablespoon superfine sugar

1½ cups ground almonds

1¼ cups confectioners' sugar

3 eggs

¼ cup all-purpose flour

2 tablespoons unsalted butter, melted

**For the coffee buttercream**

1 cup granulated sugar

2 tablespoons water

½ teaspoon vanilla extract

1 egg, plus 1 egg yolk

1¾ sticks unsalted butter

2 tablespoons espresso coffee, cooled

**For the ganache**

8 ounces semisweet chocolate, chopped

2 tablespoons unsalted butter, softened

½ cup heavy cream

½ cup milk

**For the coffee syrup**

¼ cup espresso coffee

2 tablespoons dark rum

1 teaspoon granulated sugar

**To decorate**

2 ounces semisweet chocolate, chopped

4 tablespoons unsalted butter, melted

First, make the sponge. Preheat the oven to 400°F and line two ½-inch deep, 8 x 12-inch baking sheets with parchment paper.

Use a freestanding mixer or electric handheld mixer to whisk the egg whites and superfine sugar to stiff peaks. In a separate bowl, mix together the almonds and confectioners' sugar, then add the whole eggs and whisk again until pale and doubled in volume. Sift the flour and fold in, then gently fold in the egg whites followed by the melted butter. Divide the batter between the baking sheets, tilting the pans to spread the batter evenly. Bake in the oven for 7–10 minutes, until golden and springy to the touch—watch carefully, because the sponge cooks quickly. Turn out onto cooling racks and let cool.

To make the coffee buttercream, put the sugar and water into a saucepan and heat to 250°F on a candy thermometer, if you have one, or until syrupy and almost a caramel. Add the vanilla to the syrup once the mixture thickens, then remove from the heat. In a heatproof bowl, beat together the egg and egg yolk using an electric handheld mixer, then pour on the hot syrup with the beaters still running and continue to beat until fluffy. Cool slightly, then beat in the butter. Stir in the coffee, then let cool.

To make the ganache, put the chocolate and butter into a heatproof bowl. Put the cream and milk into a saucepan and heat until steaming hot, then pass through a strainer onto the chocolate and butter. Stir until melted, smooth, and thick. Let set for a few minutes to form a spreading consistency.

Using the bottom of an 8-inch-square cake pan as a stencil, cut out a square from the sponge. Repeat with the other sponge sheet, then join together the leftover sponge and cut out a third square.

To assemble the cake, fit the first sponge square in the bottom of an 8-inch loose-bottom cake pan, 3 inches deep, then mix together the coffee syrup ingredients and brush over the sponge. Spread half of the ganache over the top, then add the sponge square made with the two halves. Brush again with coffee syrup, then spread with the coffee buttercream. Top with the final square, then brush with syrup and spread the remaining ganache over the top. Chill in the refrigerator for 30 minutes.

To decorate in the traditional French way, melt the semisweet chocolate in a bowl over a saucepan of barely simmering water, making sure the surface of the water does not touch the bowl. Stir in the melted butter, then spoon the chocolate into a small pastry bag with a small hole snipped at the tip. Pipe the word "Opéra" on top of the cake, then let set. You can also sprinkle with some gold leaf flakes for a luxurious touch, if you like. Remove the cake pan using a kitchen blowtorch or the heat of your hands.

# Hot chocolate soufflés

I love soufflé. It is such a simple recipe with few ingredients, but it still has the wow factor every time you make one. This chocolate version, especially when served with a vanilla ice cream drop, is superb.

**Serves 6**

**Preparation time:** 20 minutes

**Cooking time:** 15 minutes

unsalted butter, for greasing

4 ounces semisweet chocolate, coarsely chopped

2 teaspoon dark rum (optional)

2 tablespoons crème fraîche

4 eggs, separated, plus 2 egg whites

pinch of salt

confectioners' sugar, for dusting

Preheat the oven to 400°F. Grease six ramekin dishes.

Melt the chocolate in a heatproof bowl set over a saucepan of barely simmering water, making sure the surface of the water does not touch the bowl. Stir in the rum, if using. Remove from the heat and add the crème fraîche, then the egg yolks.

In a large, clean, dry bowl, whisk all the egg whites and the salt to soft peaks.

Fold one-quarter of the egg whites into the chocolate mixture, then fold in the remaining whites.

Fill the prepared ramekins to the top with the batter, then clean the rims using your finger and thumb. Place on a baking sheet and bake in the oven for 10–12 minutes, or until nicely risen. Dust with confectioners' sugar and serve immediately.

## Tip

For a delicious party trick, serve your soufflés with an ice cream drop. Before you make the soufflés, scoop out six balls of good-quality vanilla ice cream and place on a freezer-proof plate. Keep in the freezer until ready to serve. When serving the soufflés at the table, drop an ice cream ball into each soufflé.

# Chocolate and banana tarte tatin

This is a great winter dessert and seriously indulgent. The chocolate, caramel-infused bananas are full of flavor, and the delicate pastry simply melts in your mouth.

**Serves 6**

**Preparation time:** 15 minutes

**Cooking time:** 30–35 minutes

1 sheet ready-to-bake all-butter puff pastry

all-purpose flour, for dusting

½ cup firmly packed light brown sugar

4 tablespoons unsalted butter, plus extra for greasing

3 ounces semisweet chocolate, finely chopped

2 cinnamon sticks

5 firm bananas, cut into large chunks

Preheat the oven to 400°F. Grease an 8½-inch diameter flameproof tart pan or ovenproof skillet. Roll out the pastry on a floured surface to a circle 1inch larger than the pan. Put to one side.

Put the sugar and butter into the pan and cook gently over medium heat until it forms a dark blond caramel. Remove from the heat and add the chocolate, stirring until melted. Drop the cinnamon sticks into the center of the pan.

Arrange the banana chunks tightly in the pan. Place the pastry over the top, tucking in the overhanging edges of the pastry between the fruit and the pan. Using a small knife, pierce the top of the pastry to let the steam escape.

Bake in the oven for 25–30 minutes, or until the pastry is puffed up and golden. Turn out onto a serving dish immediately. Serve with crème fraîche or ice cream.

# Harlequin

I came across this recipe when working for chefs Michel and Albert Roux. It's a delicate combination of dark and white chocolate with whiskey and coconut. This is a great dessert and certainly worth the effort.

**Serves 8**

**Preparation time:** 1 hour, plus cooling and chilling overnight

**Cooking time:** 40–45 minutes

butter, for greasing

4 eggs

⅔ cup superfine sugar (or the same quantity of granulated sugar processed in a food processor)

3 tablespoons all-purpose flour

¼ cup unsweeetened cocoa powder

¼ cup toasted dry coconut

confectioners' sugar, for dusting

**For the white chocolate cream**

2 ounces white chocolate, coarsely chopped

1 stick unsalted butter, softened

2 cups confectioners' sugar

1 tablespoon milk

**For the semisweet chocolate cream**

5 ounces semisweet chocolate, coarsely chopped

1¼ cups heavy cream

**For the whiskey syrup**

¼ cup granulated sugar

¼ cup water

1 tablespoon whiskey

Preheat the oven to 350°F. Lightly grease two 8-inch diameter cake pans and line with parchment paper.

To make the sponge, separate two of the eggs and put the yolks and two whole eggs into a heatproof bowl with ½ cup of the sugar. Set the bowl over a saucepan of simmering water and whisk using a wire whisk until the mixture reaches 104°F on a candy thermometer. Using an electric handheld mixer, continue whisking the mixture until it doubles in volume. Sift together the flour and cocoa powder and then gently fold in.

In a clean, dry bowl, whisk the egg whites and the remaining sugar to soft peaks, then fold into the sponge mixture. Spoon into the prepared pans and bake in the oven for 20–25 minutes, or until a toothpick inserted into the centers comes out clean. Turn out onto a cooling rack to cool.

To make the white chocolate cream, melt the white chocolate in a heatproof bowl set over a saucepan of barely simmering water, making sure the surface of the water does not touch the bowl. Let cool. Beat together the butter and half of the confectioners' sugar until smooth, then add the remaining confectioners' sugar a little at a time, beating until smooth. Stir in the cooled white chocolate, add the milk, and beat for 2 minutes. Set aside.

For the semisweet chocolate cream, melt the semisweet chocolate as above. Meanwhile, whip the cream to soft peaks, then quickly whisk one-third into the hot melted chocolate. Gently fold in the remaining cream.

For the whiskey syrup, heat the sugar and water in a saucepan until the sugar has dissolved. Boil for 4 minutes, then let cool before stirring in the whiskey.

To assemble the cake, slice the sponges horizontally into ¼-inch-thick circles. You will need only three of the sponges (keep the remaining sponge for another recipe). Fit a layer of sponge in the bottom of an 8½-inch diameter deep loose-bottom cake pan. Drizzle one-third of the whiskey syrup over the sponge, then sprinkle with a little coconut. Spread half of the semisweet chocolate cream on top. Add a second layer of sponge, drizzle with another third of the syrup, and sprinkle with coconut. Spread with all the white chocolate cream. Top with the third sponge, drizzle with the remaining syrup and sprinkle with more coconut. Spread with the remaining semisweet chocolate cream right to the top of the pan and smooth, using a spatula, then sprinkle coconut over the top. Let set in the refrigerator overnight.

One hour before serving, remove the cake from the refrigerator and remove the pan using a kitchen blowtorch or the heat of your hands. Dust with confectioners' sugar before serving.

# Double-baked chocolate meringue brownie

This is an incredible recipe! The texture of the two contrasting layers, one gooey and rich and the other crunchy with a marshmallow center, makes this recipe really special.

**Serves 8**
**Preparation time:** 25 minutes
**Cooking time:** 1 hour 10 minutes

**For the brownie**

2 sticks unsalted butter, plus extra for greasing

12 ounces semisweet chocolate, coarsely chopped

1½ cups firmly packed light brown sugar

5 extra-large eggs, separated

**For the chocolate meringue**

4 egg whites

1 cup plus 2 tablespoons superfine sugar (or the same quantity of granulated sugar processed in a food processor)

2 teaspoons vanilla extract

1 teaspoon cornstarch

⅔ cup unsweetened cocoa powder

Preheat the oven to 350°F. Grease an 8½-inch diameter springform cake pan and line with parchment paper, making sure the paper is at least 2 inches above the rim of the pan.

To make the brownie, melt the butter and chocolate in a heatproof bowl set over a saucepan of barely simmering water, making sure the surface of the water does not touch the bowl. Add the sugar, stirring until it has completely dissolved. Remove from the heat and add the egg yolks.

In a clean, dry bowl, whisk the egg whites to soft peaks. Fold a couple of tablespoons of the egg whites into the chocolate mixture, then fold in the remaining whites using a rubber spatula. Spoon the batter into the prepared pan and bake in the oven for 40 minutes.

Meanwhile, make the meringue. In a large, clean, dry bowl, whisk the egg whites to stiff peaks, adding the sugar a little at a time, then add the vanilla extract. Sift together the cornstarch and cocoa powder, then fold into the meringue until the mixture is even and glossy.

Remove the chocolate brownie from the oven and cover the top with the meringue. Return to the oven for another 25 minutes, or until the meringue puffs up and a crust forms on the top but the center is still soft. Let cool in the pan. The center will collapse slightly. Serve warm with crème fraîche or vanilla ice cream.

# Chocolate and chestnut truffle cakes

One of my favorite areas of France is Lozère, a mountain region with a great food legacy. Chestnuts are popular in both cooking and baking, and are used to make chestnut flour, which is gluten free. The flavor of chestnuts goes well with chocolate.

**Serves 6**

**Preparation time:** 15 minutes

**Cooking time:** 25 minutes

4 ounces semisweet chocolate, coarsely chopped

1 stick unsalted butter, plus extra for greasing

2⅓ cups sweetened chestnut spread

1 teaspoon vanilla paste or extract

2 tablespoons chestnut flour

4 eggs, separated

chopped candied chestnuts, to decorate

Preheat the oven to 350°F. Grease six individual 4-inch diameter loose-bottom tart pans and line the bottoms with parchment paper.

Gently melt the chocolate and butter in a heatproof bowl set over a saucepan of barely simmering water, making sure the surface of the water does not touch the bowl.

Remove from the heat and stir in the chestnut spread and vanilla. Add the flour, then beat in the egg yolks one at a time. In a clean, dry bowl, whisk the egg whites to soft peaks, then fold into the chestnut mixture.

Divide the batter between the prepared pans, filling them three-quarters full. Bake in the oven for 18–20 minutes, or until a toothpick inserted into the centers comes out clean. Let cool in the pans for 5 minutes, then remove and transfer onto serving plates. Serve warm, decorated with candied chestnuts and drizzled with honey, with cream alongside for pouring over the top.

## Tip

Sweetened chestnut spread or paste (crème de marrons) is available canned from good delicatessens, some larger supermarkets, and online.

# Chocolate omelet soufflé

Not far from where I grew up in France there is a restaurant, at Mont Saint-Michel, famous for its sweet omelet soufflé. This is my take on Madame Poulard's secret recipe.

**Serves 1**

**Preparation time:** 10 minutes

**Cooking time:** 10 minutes

1¾ cups fresh mixed berries, such as raspberries, red currants, or blueberries

2 teaspoons raspberry preserves

1 ounce semisweet chocolate, coarsely chopped

1 egg yolk

1½ tablespoons superfine sugar, plus an extra 2 teaspoons (or the same quantity of granulated sugar processed in a food processor for 1 minute)

1 teaspoon vanilla paste or extract

2 egg whites

1 tablespoons unsalted butter

confectioners' sugar, for dusting

Put the berries and preserves into a saucepan and cook over medium heat for 1 minute, or until the berries start to puff up. Remove from the heat and put aside.

Melt the chocolate in a heatproof bowl set over a saucepan of barely simmering water, making sure the surface of the water does not touch the bowl.

Put the egg yolk, the 2 teaspoons of superfine sugar, and the vanilla into a bowl and mix together, then stir in the chocolate.

In a clean, dry bowl, whisk the egg whites to stiff peaks, adding the remaining superfine sugar a little at a time. Fold one-quarter of the egg whites into the chocolate to loosen the mixture, then fold in the remaining whites.

Melt the butter in a small 6½-inch diameter flameproof nonstick skillet over medium heat, and meanwhile preheat the broiler to medium-high. Spoon the chocolate mixture into the skillet, making sure it is an even layer, and cook for 2–3 minutes, then place under the broiler for 1 minute, or until set, making sure it does not burn.

Spoon the berry mixture over one half of the omelet. Fold the omelet over to enclose the filling, then dust with confectioners' sugar. Serve immediately.

## Tip

Use egg whites at room temperature to get the most volume when whisking.

# White chocolate and passion fruit cheesecake

I am a big fan of the baked cheesecake, and this recipe is smooth and zesty with a touch of the exotic. It's perfectly sweetened with the white chocolate—a great summer dessert.

**Serves 6**

**Preparation time:** 30 minutes, plus cooling and chilling overnight

**Cooking time:** 1 hour 5 minutes– 1 hour 15 minutes

1 cup crushed graham crackers

4 tablespoons unsalted butter, melted, plus extra for greasing

4 ounces white chocolate, chopped

½ cup light cream

1 cup cream cheese, softened

1 cup mascarpone cheese

¼ cup granulated sugar

2 teaspoons vanilla extract

4 eggs, separated

½ cup passion fruit pulp, strained to remove the seeds

passion fruit, to decorate

Preheat the oven to 350°F. Grease an 8-inch diameter springform cake pan.

Put the crushed cookies and melted butter into a bowl and mix well. Transfer the mixture to the prepared pan and press down with the back of a spoon. Bake in the oven for 10 minutes, or until golden. Let cool. Reduce the oven temperature to 300°F.

Put the chocolate into a heatproof bowl. Put the cream into a small saucepan and heat until steaming hot, but do not let it boil. Pour the cream onto the chocolate and stir until smooth. Put to one side.

In a separate bowl, beat together the cream cheese and mascarpone until smooth. Add the sugar, vanilla, and egg yolks. Stir in the white chocolate mixture and passion fruit pulp.

In a large, clean, dry bowl, whisk two egg whites to soft peaks (save the remaining two egg whites for another recipe). Fold a large spoonful of the egg whites into the batter vigorously, then gently fold in the remaining whites until smooth.

Spoon the mixture onto the cooled crust and bake for 50–60 minutes, or until set but with a slight wobble in the center. Turn off the oven and let the cheesecake cool inside the oven for 2 hours with the door ajar. Chill in the refrigerator overnight.

Remove from the pan and decorate with fresh passion fruit quarters.

# Chocolate coffee baked cheesecake

Cheesecakes are always popular and I have to say I am a great fan of a baked cheesecake. The chocolate in this recipe is enhanced by the addition of the rich, strong coffee flavor.

**Serves 6–8**

**Preparation time:** 30 minutes, plus chilling and cooling

**Cooking time:** 1 hour 35 minutes

1½ cups crushed chocolate cookies

4 tablespoons unsalted butter, melted, plus extra for greasing

1 cup cream cheese

1 cup mascarpone cheese

½ cup granulated sugar

⅔ cup heavy cream

1 teaspoon vanilla paste or extract

1 tablespoon all-purpose flour

2 eggs, plus 1 egg yolk

1 teaspoon instant coffee

2 teaspoons hot water

2 teaspoons coffee extract

pure cocoa powder, for dusting

**For the chocolate topping**

1 stick unsalted butter

1 tablespoon crème fraîche

¼ cup light brown sugar

5 ounces semisweet chocolate, finely chopped

1 teaspoon coffee extract

Preheat the oven to 300°F. Grease an 8½-inch diameter springform cake pan.

Put the crushed cookies and melted butter into a bowl and mix well. Transfer the mixture into the prepared pan and press down with the back of a spoon. Let set in the refrigerator for 15 minutes.

Put the cream cheese, mascarpone, sugar, cream, vanilla, and flour into a large bowl and beat together until nice and smooth. Beat in the eggs and egg yolk. Dissolve the coffee in the hot water, then beat into the mixture with the coffee extract.

Spoon the batter onto the chilled crust and bake in the oven for 1 hour 30 minutes, or until set but still with a slight wobble in the center. Turn off the oven and let the cheesecake cool inside the oven for 2 hours with the door ajar. Chill in the refrigerator.

To make the chocolate topping, put the butter, crème fraîche, and sugar into a small saucepan and heat gently until melted. Add the chocolate and coffee extract and heat gently for another 2 minutes, stirring continuously. Remove from the heat, then give the mixture a good whisk. Let cool for a few minutes, then pour over the chilled cheesecake. Return to the refrigerator and let set.

Remove from the pan and dust generously with cocoa powder. Serve with whipped vanilla cream.

# Proper Black Forest gateau

This cake has a kitsch reputation, but when done properly it is extremely delicious and light, and will take you on a trip down memory lane.

**Serves 10**

**Preparation time:** 45 minutes, plus cooling

**Cooking time:** 30–35 minutes

6 eggs

1 teaspoon vanilla extract

1¼ cups granulated sugar

⅔ cup unsweetened cocoa powder

¾ cup all-purpose flour

1¼ sticks unsalted butter, melted and cooled, plus extra for greasing

5 ounces semisweet chocolate

3 tablespoons raspberry preserves

40 fresh black cherries, pitted (or canned cherries, drained)

confectioners' sugar, for dusting

**For the syrup**

1 cup water

1 cup granulated sugar

2 tablespoons kirsch

**For the kirsch cream**

3 cups heavy cream

⅓ cup superfine sugar (or the same quantity of granulated sugar processed in a food processor for 1 minute)

2 teaspoons vanilla extract

3 tablespoons kirsch

First make the sponge. Preheat the oven to 350°F. Grease three 8½-inch diameter cake pans and line the bottoms with parchment paper.

In a large bowl, beat together the eggs, vanilla, and sugar, using an electric handheld mixer, until thick and the beaters leave a trail when lifted above the mixture. Sift together the cocoa powder and flour, then fold in. Stir in the melted butter.

Divide the cake batter among the prepared pans and bake in the oven for 20–25 minutes, or until springy to the touch. Let cool in the pans for 5 minutes, then turn out onto a cooling rack to cool completely.

Meanwhile, shave the block of chocolate by using a vegetable peeler or by carefully scraping the blade of a large kitchen knife across the surface of the chocolate. Keep the chocolate shavings in the refrigerator until needed.

To make the syrup, put the water and sugar in a saucepan and bring to a boil, then boil for 5 minutes. Let cool, then add the kirsch.

To make the kirsch cream, whip the cream and sugar to firm peaks, then fold in the vanilla and kirsch.

To assemble the cake, level the tops of the sponges, if necessary, using a sharp knife. Place a little kirsch cream on a serving plate and secure one of the sponges on top. Brush the sponge with some of the syrup, then spread over the raspberry preserves. Sandwich together with a second sponge and brush again with the syrup. Spread over a thick layer of the kirsch cream, about ½ inch deep. Cover with the cherries, reserving eight for decoration. Spread a little more cream over the cherries to secure them, then top with the final sponge, upside down to create an even, flat surface. Brush with the remaining syrup.

Spoon ⅓ cup of the kirsch cream into a pastry bag fitted with a large star tip and set aside. Using a spatula, cover the top and side of the cake with the remaining cream. Carefully stick the chocolate shavings all over the side of the cake with the palm of your hand. Pipe around the edge of the cake and eight swirls in the middle, then place the reserved cherries on top of the swirls. Serve dusted with confectioners' sugar.

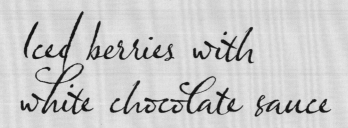

# Iced berries with white chocolate sauce

Inspired by a birthday meal at The Ivy restaurant in London, this is a really delicious, last-minute, refreshing summer dessert.

**Serves 6**

**Preparation time:** 10 minutes, plus chilling

**Cooking time:** 5 minutes

4 cups mixed frozen berries (about 1 pound)

⅔ cup heavy cream

5 ounces white chocolate, coarsely chopped

1 teaspoon vanilla extract

2 tablespoons white rum (optional)

Put the frozen berries into the refrigerator 1 hour before serving so that they soften but are still icy.

To make the sauce, put the cream, chocolate, and vanilla into a small saucepan and heat gently, stirring continuously, until the chocolate has melted. Let cool for 2 minutes, then stir in the rum, if using.

Divide the berries among six shallow bowls and pour the hot sauce over them. Serve immediately before the fruits completely defrost.

## Tip

Use a mixture of blackberries, blueberries, and raspberries along with red currants—if you can get them—for a perfect summer dessert.

# French bistro chocolate mousse

One of my favorite bistros in Paris is called Chez Janou. Apart from the great atmosphere, the best thing there is the chocolate mousse made the old-fashion way and served in a large earthenware vat with a ladle—and you can eat as much as you want. A dream!

**Serves 6**

**Preparation time:** 15 minutes, plus chilling

**Cooking time:** 5 minutes

8 ounces semisweet chocolate, coarsely chopped

5 tablespoons unsalted butter

6 eggs, separated

pinch of salt

Melt the chocolate and butter in a heatproof bowl set over a saucepan of barely simmering water, making sure the surface of the water does not touch the bowl. Remove from the heat, then beat in the egg yolks.

In a large, clean, dry bowl, whisk the egg whites and salt to stiff peaks. Fold a large spoonful of the egg whites into the chocolate mixture to loosen, then gently fold in the remaining whites.

Pour the mixture into a serving dish, cover with plastic wrap, and chill in the refrigerator for at least 4 hours. See previous page for the finished result. The mousse is lovely served with Breton Shortbread with Chocolate (see page 56).

## Tip

For a grown-up version, add a little orange liqueur, amaretto liqueur, or Cognac to the mixture.

# Chocolate "samosas"

These unusually sweet samosas are great for a party to serve as a canapé, or even as a dessert with some exotic ice cream, such as mango ice cream.

**Makes 4**

**Preparation time:** 10 minutes

**Cooking time:** 10 minutes

2 tablespoons unsalted butter

2 ripe bananas, sliced

1 tablespoon packed light brown sugar

2 sheets of phyllo pastry

2 ounces semisweet chocolate, finely grated

½ teaspoon ground cinnamon

Melt half the butter in a skillet, add the banana slices and sugar, and sauté for about 4–5 minutes, or until the bananas have caramelized, turning them over halfway during cooking.

Cut the pastry sheets in half. Place banana slices and a good sprinkling of chocolate and cinnamon toward one end of each pastry sheet, then fold up to resemble a triangular "samosa" shape.

Heat the remaining butter in the skillet over medium heat, add the pastries, and cook for about 2 minutes on each side, or until golden brown all over. Serve immediately.

# Chocolate and framboise roulade

This recipe is inspired by my mentors Albert and Michel Roux's classic recipe Le Roule Marquis, which I used to bake when working for them. This easy-to-make recipe is light and contains no flour, making it a perfect dessert for a casual lunch or dinner.

**Serves 10**

**Preparation time:** 35 minutes, plus cooling and chilling

**Cooking time:** 25 minutes

¼ cup granulated sugar

¼ cup water

2 tablespoons crème de framboise or raspberry liqueur

1¼ cups heavy cream

⅓ cup confectioners' sugar

4 cups fresh raspberries, plus extra to decorate

**For the sponge**

butter, for greasing

6 ounces semisweet chocolate, coarsely chopped

6 eggs, separated

¾ cup plus 2 tablespoons granulated sugar

1 teaspoon vanilla paste or extract

2 tablespoons unsweetened cocoa powder, sifted

First make the sponge. Preheat the oven to 350°F. Lightly grease a 15 x 11-inch baking pan and line with parchment paper.

Melt the chocolate in a heatproof bowl set over a saucepan of barely simmering water, making sure the surface of the water does not touch the bowl. Let cool for a few minutes.

In a large bowl, beat together the sugar and egg yolks, using an electric handheld mixer, until pale and creamy. Add the vanilla paste and cooled chocolate and stir until smooth. In a large, clean, dry bowl, whisk the egg whites to stiff peaks. Stir a large spoonful of the egg whites into the chocolate mixture, mixing gently, then fold in the remaining whites. Fold in the cocoa powder.

Spoon the batter into the prepared pan and gently level the top using a spatula. Bake in the oven for 18–20 minutes, or until firm to the touch. Place a sheet of nonstick parchment paper on top of the sponge, then put a clean, damp dish towel on top of the paper. Let cool completely.

Meanwhile, make a syrup by putting the granulated sugar and water into a small saucepan and heating gently until the sugar has dissolved. Boil for 2 minutes, then turn off the heat and let cool completely before stirring in the framboise.

To assemble the roulade, whip the cream until it just holds its shape. Dust a large piece of nonstick parchment paper with some of the confectioners' sugar, then turn the roulade out onto it and peel off the lining paper. Brush the framboise syrup over the cooled sponge, then spread over the whipped cream and cover with the raspberries, pushing them into the cream slightly.

Starting from a long edge, roll up the sponge like a jelly roll. Roll tightly to start with and use the paper to help you roll it up. The roulade may crack when you do this, but that's part of its charm! Chill in the refrigerator for at least 4 hours.

To serve, trim the ends of the roulade and place on a long serving plate. Dust generously with the remaining confectioners' sugar and serve with extra raspberries. I like to serve this light dessert with a raspberry coulis.

# Chocolate "cassis" royale

This is the perfect dessert for a special occasion or get-together. It's one of my favorite combinations, but blueberries are just as good as black currants.

**Serves 8**

**Preparation time:** 40 minutes, plus cooling and chilling overnight

**Cooking time:** 40–45 minutes

butter, for greasing

8 ounces semisweet chocolate, coarsely chopped

3 eggs, plus 2 egg yolks

1 teaspoon cornstarch

3 egg whites

1½ cups granulated sugar

1¼ cups balsamic vinegar

2⅔ cups fresh black currants or blueberries

**For the chocolate mousse**

8 ounces semisweet chocolate, coarsely chopped

5 egg whites

pinch of salt

**For the glaze**

8 ounces semisweet chocolate, chopped

8 ounces white chocolate, chopped

½ cup milk

⅓ cup light cream

¼ cup granulated sugar

¼ cup light corn syrup

First make the sponge. Preheat the oven to 350°F. Grease two 8-inch diameter cake pans and line with parchment paper.

Melt the chocolate in a heatproof bowl set over a saucepan of barely simmering water, making sure the surface of the water does not touch the bowl. Stir together the whole eggs and egg yolks in a bowl, then whisk into the melted chocolate with the cornstarch. In a clean, dry bowl, whisk the egg whites to soft peaks. Fold a large spoonful of the egg whites into the chocolate mixture to loosen, then gently fold in the remaining whites.

Divide the batter between the prepared pans and bake in the oven for 20–25 minutes, or until a toothpick inserted into the centers comes out clean. Let cool in the pans for 5 minutes before turning out onto a cooling rack to cool completely.

Meanwhile, make a syrup. Put the sugar and vinegar into a saucepan and bring to a boil, then simmer until it forms a thick syrup—almost a caramel. Remove from the heat and put to one side.

To make the chocolate mousse, melt the chocolate as above. In a large, clean, dry bowl, whisk the egg whites and salt to stiff peaks. Fold a good spoonful of the egg whites into the melted chocolate to loosen, then gently fold in the remaining whites.

To assemble the cake, slice the sponges in half horizontally. You will only need three of the sponge layers (keep the remaining layer for another recipe). Fit a layer of sponge in the bottom of an 8-inch diameter, deep, loose-bottom cake pan. Cover with the berries. Reheat the syrup and drizzle it all over the fruits, covering them completely. Add a second layer of sponge on top and press down. Spread with the chocolate mousse, leaving enough space for the third sponge on top. If there is any chocolate mousse left, spread it over the top of the sponge using a spatula. Let set in the refrigerator overnight.

When ready to serve, make the glaze. Put the dark and white chocolates into separate heatproof bowls. Put the milk, cream, sugar, and corn syrup in a saucepan and bring to a boil. Remove from the heat and pour half over each bowl of chocolate, stirring until it has completely melted.

Remove the cake from the refrigerator and remove from the pan, using a kitchen blowtorch or the heat of your hands, then place it on a cooling rack set over a large plate or baking sheet. Pour the chocolate glazes on top, letting them drip down the side to cover it completely. Use a spatula to swirl into a marble effect and smooth evenly, then serve.

# Milk, semisweet, and white chocolate verrines

Serving desserts in small shot glasses is a popular trend, especially for parties and functions. This trio of chocolate looks great and, of course, tastes great, too.

**Serves 8 or fills 20 shot glasses**

**Preparation time:** 35 minutes, plus chilling

**Cooking time:** 25 minutes

**For the semisweet chocolate layer**

3 ounces semisweet chocolate, coarsely chopped

1 tablespoon granulated sugar

2 eggs, separated

**For the milk chocolate layer**

3 ounces milk chocolate, coarsely chopped

1½ teaspoons granulated sugar

2 eggs, separated

**For the white chocolate layer**

2 egg yolks

2 teaspoons granulated sugar

1 teaspoon cold water

5 ounces white chocolate, coarsely chopped

1 cup heavy cream

Start with the semisweet chocolate layer. Melt the chocolate and sugar in a heatproof bowl set over a saucepan of barely simmering water, making sure the surface of the water does not touch the bowl. Remove from the heat and stir in the egg yolks. In a clean, dry bowl, whisk the egg whites to firm peaks, then fold into the chocolate mixture. Divide the mixture evenly among glasses or shot glasses. Let set in the refrigerator.

Next, make the milk chocolate layer as above. Carefully pour it over the set layer in the glasses and return to the refrigerator to set.

Finally, make the white chocolate layer. Put the egg yolks, sugar, and water into a heatproof bowl and mix together. Set the bowl over a saucepan of simmering water and beat for 10 minutes using an electric handheld mixer. Remove from the heat and continue to beat until the mixture is thick and creamy.

Melt the white chocolate in separate heatproof bowl set over the simmering water, then let cool for a few minutes. Lightly whip the cream to soft peaks. Stir the cooled chocolate into the egg mixture, then fold in the whipped cream. Carefully pour the mixture over the set layer in the glasses and chill in the refrigerator for at least 6 hours until completely set. Serve decorated with grated chocolate.

# Black currant and vanilla crème brûlée chocolate cake

I love finding surprises when I cut into a cake or dessert. It could be a texture, liquid, or, as in this case, a soft and smooth vanilla crème brûlée encased in a black currant-flavor chocolate mousse.

**Serves 8**

**Preparation time:** 50 minutes, plus cooling and freezing overnight

**Cooking time:** 50 minutes

butter, for greasing

3 tablespoons granulated sugar, plus 1 tablespoon for sprinkling

2 egg yolks

1 cup heavy cream

1 vanilla bean, split lengthwise

1 (8-inch) diameter, ¼-inch deep chocolate sponge cake (use any chocolate sponge recipe)

¼ cup black currant or blueberry preserves

**For the chocolate mousse**

¼ cup water

¼ cup granulated sugar

2 black currant or blueberry tea bags

8 ounces semisweet chocolate, coarsely chopped

1¾ cups heavy cream

6 egg yolks

**For the ganache**

½ cup heavy cream

4 ounces semisweet chocolate, chopped

2 tablespoons unsalted butter

Preheat the oven to 225°F. Lightly grease an 8-inch diameter ovenproof dish (the dish must be slightly smaller than your cake ring or pan) and sprinkle it with the 1 tablespoon of sugar.

To make the crème brûlée, put the egg yolks and remaining sugar into a heatproof bowl and mix together. Pour the cream into a saucepan, add the vanilla bean, and bring to a boil. Remove from the heat and pass the hot cream through a fine strainer onto the egg mixture, stirring continuously. Pour the mixture into the prepared dish and cook in the oven for 30 minutes, or until lightly set. Let cool, then freeze for 2 hours.

Meanwhile, make the mousse. Put the water, sugar, and tea bags into a saucepan over high heat and bring to a boil, stirring until the sugar has dissolved. Remove from the heat and let the syrup steep.

Melt the chocolate in a heatproof bowl set over a saucepan of barely simmering water, making sure the surface of the water does not touch the bowl. Let cool. Whip the cream to soft peaks. Squeeze the syrup from the tea bags and bring back to a boil. In a large bowl, beat the egg yolks, using an electric handheld mixer, then pour in the syrup and continue beating the mixture until it is light and fluffy. Let cool, then stir into the cooled chocolate. Fold in the whipped cream.

To assemble the cake, slice the chocolate sponge in half horizontally and brush each layer with black currant preserves. Place an 8½-inch diameter ring or springform cake pan on a baking sheet and fit a layer of sponge in the bottom, preserves side up. Spread with half of the chocolate mousse.

Turn out the crème brûlée and place on top of the mousse. Spread with the remaining mousse and top with the remaining sponge, preserves side down. Return to the freezer to set for several hours or overnight.

To make the ganache, put the cream into a saucepan and heat gently, then carefully stir in the chocolate until melted and smooth. Remove from the heat. Cut the butter into small pieces and add to the chocolate mixture, stirring continuously until thoroughly incorporated.

Remove the frozen dessert from the ring or pan, using a kitchen blowtorch or the heat of your hands, and place it on a cooling rack set over a large plate or baking sheet. Pour the warm ganache over it, smooth with a spatula, and let set. Serve at room temperature.

# White chocolate tiramisu

The Italian classic and now international sensation, revisited by me with the addition of exotic cardamom, coffee, and white chocolate. This recipe is best made the day before serving.

**Serves 6**

**Preparation time:** 25 minutes, plus chilling overnight

**Cooking time:** 5 minutes

butter, for greasing

¼ cup unsweetened cocoa powder

2 teaspoon ground cardamom

½ cup hot black coffee

6 ounces white chocolate, coarsely chopped

1 cup mascarpone cheese

3 eggs, separated

pinch of salt

13 speculoos cookies (see the tip below)

confectioners' sugar, for dusting

Grease six ramekin dishes, then dust with some of the cocoa powder.

Add the cardamom to the hot black coffee and let steep while it cools.

Melt the chocolate in a heatproof bowl set over a saucepan of barely simmering water, making sure the surface of the water does not touch the bowl.

Put the mascarpone in a large bowl and beat in the egg yolks. Stir in the melted chocolate. In a clean, dry bowl, whisk the egg whites and salt to soft peaks, then gently fold into the mascarpone mixture.

Dunk six cookies into the spiced coffee, one at a time, and place one in each of the ramekins. Add a layer of the mascarpone mixture. Repeat with another layer of dipped cookies, then finally top with a layer of mascarpone.

Crumble the remaining cookie and sprinkle a little on the top of each ramekin. Chill in the refrigerator overnight. Serve dusted with the remaining cocoa powder and some confectioners' sugar.

## Tip

Speculoos cookies are thin, very crunchy cookies originally from the Netherlands, and are now available in larger supermarkets, specialty food stores, and online, sometimes sold as Dutch windmill cookies or Biscoff cookies.

# White chocolate, raspberry, and lemon Battenberg

This is my take on a great British cake, making it lighter, colorful, and a touch more contemporary in presentation, too.

**Serves 8**

**Preparation time:** 45 minutes, plus cooling

**Cooking time:** 30–35 minutes

3 sticks unsalted butter, softened, plus extra for greasing

1¾ cups granulated sugar

2¼ cups all-purpose flour

1 cup ground almonds (almond meal)

1 tablespoon baking powder

6 eggs

1 teaspoon vanilla paste or extract

2 tablespoons milk

2 tablespoons freeze-dried raspberry pieces

2 teaspoons raspberry extract

few drops of pink food coloring

2 teaspoons lemon extract

few drops of yellow food coloring

½ cup raspberry preserves

confectioners' sugar, for dusting

10 ounces white modeling chocolate

fresh raspberries, to decorate

Preheat the oven to 350°F. Grease two 8-inch-square cake pans or a Battenberg pan and line with parchment paper.

Put the butter, granulated sugar, flour, ground almonds, baking powder, eggs, vanilla, and milk into a large bowl and beat together until smooth. Divide the batter in half and put one half into another bowl. Mix the dried raspberries, raspberry extract, and pink food coloring into one batter until a pink color. Mix the lemon extract and yellow food coloring into the other batter until you get a nice bright yellow color.

Spoon each batter into a prepared pan and bake in the oven for 25–30 minutes, or until a toothpick inserted into the centers comes out clean. Let cool in the pans.

Heat the raspberry preserves in a small saucepan until runny, then pass through a strainer into a bowl. Trim the sponges, each to the same width as the sponge height, to form four identical long rectangles, two from each color (freeze any leftover sponge for another time). Using a patterned rolling pin on a work surface lightly dusted with confectioners' sugar, roll out the white modeling chocolate to a rectangle, 10 x 8 inches.

Place a pink and yellow sponge rectangle side by side, brushing some preserves in between them to stick together. Brush some preserves over the top, then place the remaining pink and yellow sponges on top, alternating the colors and sticking together with more preserves. Brush the outside of the sponges with preserves but not the cut ends.

Carefully place the stacked sponge pieces in the center of the modeling chocolate, then tightly wrap the chocolate around the cake. Turn it over so that it is seam side down and trim off any excess. Dust a few fresh raspberries with confectioners' sugar and arrange on top to decorate.

## Tip

If the sponges are baked the day before the cake is assembled, they will be less prone to crumble.

# Decadent chocolate pavlova

I discovered the pavlova, a meringue-base dessert, when I arrived in the UK and ever since I have been creating new versions of this versatile, delicious dessert. This is my latest one—a chocolate version, of course!

**Serves 10**

**Preparation time:** 25 minutes, plus cooling

**Cooking time:** 1 hour 45 minutes

6 egg whites

1¾ cups superfine sugar (or the same quantity of granulated sugar processed in a food processor for 1 minute)

1 tablespoon cornstarch

¼ cup unsweetened cocoa powder

1 teaspoon white wine vinegar

½ cup semisweet chocolate chips

½ cup white chocolate chips

2 cups miniature marshmallows

2 cups heavy cream

2 teaspoons vanilla extract

2 ounces semisweet chocolate, finely grated

confectioners' sugar, for dusting

Preheat the oven to 250°F. Line a large baking sheet with parchment paper.

In a large, clean, dry bowl, whisk the egg whites to stiff peaks, adding the sugar a little at a time. Sift together the cornstarch and cocoa powder, then gently fold into the egg whites with the vinegar until combined. Fold in the chocolate chips and marshmallows but do not overmix.

Using a rubber spatula, spread some of the mixture onto the prepared baking sheet to form an 8½-inch diameter circle, then pile up with the remaining mixture.

Bake in the oven for 1 hour 45 minutes, or until crunchy on the outside and gooey in the center. Let cool on the paper and transfer to a cooling rack to cool completely. It will sink and crack a little.

Whip together the cream and vanilla to firm peaks, then pile high on the meringue. Dust with the grated chocolate and confectioners' sugar. Serve immediately.

## Tip

Use a baking sheet that is large enough to for an 8½-inch diameter meringue to expand during cooking.

# Chocolate lava cakes with orange and muscat compote

Sinfully sweet and intensely indulgent, this recipe is a chocoholic's dream! The orange compote marries the classic chocolate and orange combination.

**Serves 4**

**Preparation time:** 15 minutes

**Cooking time:** 15 minutes

2 teaspoons unsweetened cocoa powder

1 stick unsalted butter, plus extra for greasing

8 ounces semisweet chocolate, coarsely chopped

⅓ cup granulated sugar

2 eggs, plus 2 egg yolks

3 tablespoons all-purpose flour

**For the orange compote**

1 large orange, peeled and segmented

2 teaspoons granulated sugar

1 teaspoon cornstarch

½ cup muscat wine

Preheat the oven to 350°F. Grease four ⅔-cup individual dessert molds, then coat with the cocoa powder, tapping out any excess. Transfer the molds to a baking sheet.

Melt the chocolate and butter in a heatproof bowl set over a saucepan of barely simmering water, making sure the surface of the water does not touch the bowl, stirring until smooth. Let cool for a few minutes.

In a large bowl, beat together the sugar, eggs, and egg yolks, using an electric handheld mixer, until thick, pale, and fluffy and doubled in volume. Gently stir the cooled chocolate into the mixture, then fold in the flour.

Divide the batter between the prepared dessert molds, filling them three-quarters full. Cook in the oven for 12 minutes.

Meanwhile, make the orange compote. Put the orange segments into a skillet and heat gently, then stir in the sugar and cook gently until the mixture starts to sizzle. Mix the cornstarch with a little water to a paste, then add with the wine to the oranges and cook until the compote has reduced by half.

Remove the lava cakes from the oven and use a sharp knife to slide around the edge of each dessert mold to release. Turn out onto four plates and carefully remove the molds. Serve immediately with the orange compote.

# White chocolate strawberry tarts

I think this recipe shouts of summer—buttery pastry, sweet strawberry compote, light and decadent white chocolate Chantilly (a sweetened whipped cream), and flavorsome seasonal strawberries …

**Serves 6**

**Preparation time:** 20 minutes, plus cooling

**Cooking time:** 10 minutes

**For the pastry**

2 cups, plus 6 tablespoons all-purpose flour, plus extra for dusting

4 tablespoons superfine sugar

1¾ sticks unsalted butter, chopped into pieces

2 egg yolks

2 tablespoons cold water

2 teaspoons vanilla paste or extract

**For the compote**

¼ cup granulated sugar

1⅓ cups hulled and finely chopped strawberries

1 teaspoon vanilla extract

**For the Chantilly cream**

4 ounces white chocolate, coarsely chopped

1 cup heavy cream

1 cup hulled and halved strawberries, to decorate

First make the pastry. Sift the flour into a large mixing bowl and stir in the sugar. Using your fingertips, rub in the butter until the mixture resembles bread crumbs. Make a well in the center and add the rest of the ingredients. Again using your fingertips, mix together to make a smooth dough. Turn out on to a floured surface and gather together into a ball. Cover with plastic wrap and chill for at least 30 minutes before using.

Lightly grease 6 x 4 inch diameter individual tart pans. Roll out the pastry and use it to line the tins. Prick the base of each pastry shell, then chill in the refrigerator for 15 minutes.

Line each pastry shell with parchment paper and fill with pie weights. Bake in a preheated oven, 350°F, for 8–10 minutes, or until the shells are just set, then remove the paper and weights and cook empty for a further 4–5 minutes, or until the bases are dry and crisp. Remove from the pans once cool.

To make the compote, put the sugar and chopped strawberries into a saucepan and cook over medium heat until the fruits turn to a thick compote, then stir in the vanilla. Let cool.

To make the Chantilly cream, melt the white chocolate in a heatproof bowl set over a saucepan of barely simmering water, making sure the surface of the water does not touch the bowl. Let cool for a few minutes. Meanwhile, whip the cream to soft peaks, then fold one-quarter of the cream into the cooled chocolate. Fold in the remaining cream without overmixing.

To assemble the tarts, spoon some compote onto the bottom of each tart and spread with the Chantilly cream, then top with the halved strawberries.

# Mini chocolate syrup cakes

Theses cute cakes are perfect winter warmers and a great ending to a long, lazy Sunday lunch. The amaretto gives them a delicious European touch. Best served with a semisweet chocolate sauce (see page 168).

**Serves 6**

**Preparation time:** 25 minutes

**Cooking time:** 25–30 minutes

1 stick unsalted butter, plus extra for greasing

4 ounces semisweet chocolate, coarsely chopped

2 eggs

¼ cup firmly packed dark brown sugar

2½ tablespoons light corn syrup

¾ cup ground almonds (almond meal)

2 tablespoons all-purpose flour, plus extra for dusting

½ teaspoon baking powder

2 tablespoons amaretto liqueur

6 amaretti cookies, plus extra to decorate

Grease six ⅔-cup individual dessert molds and dust with flour, tapping out any excess. Cut out six small circles of parchment paper to fit the bottoms and drop one into each mold. Grease six pieces of aluminum foil, each about 6-inch square.

Put the butter and chocolate into a saucepan and heat gently until melted. Let cool.

Beat together the eggs, sugar, and light corn syrup in a large bowl, using an electric handheld mixer, until thick and foamy. Fold in the cooled chocolate mixture using a rubber spatula. Mix together the ground almonds, flour, and baking powder in a separate bowl, then fold into the mixture with 1 tablespoon of the amaretto.

Preheat the oven to 400°F.

Put the cookies in a small bowl and splash with the remaining amaretto. Fill the prepared dessert molds one-third full with cake batter, then drop a soaked cookie into each. Top with the remaining batter, leaving ½ inch between the batter and the top of the molds. Loosely scrunch a foil square over the top of each mold.

Put the molds into a roasting pan and pour in hot water to come about halfway up the sides of the molds. Bake in the oven for 20–25 minutes, or until a toothpick inserted into the centers comes out clean.

To serve the cakes, use a sharp knife to slide around the edge of each dessert mold to release. Turn out onto plates and carefully remove the molds. Spoon over some chocolate sauce, letting it drizzle over the edges, then sprinkle with broken amaretti cookies. Serve immediately.

*Old-fashioned dusted truffles*

Truffles & Treats

# Old-fashioned dusted truffles

I have fond memories of this simple but delicious recipe. As kids, we spent hours making truffles for the festive season. By the end, we were covered head to toe with cocoa powder, but it was still loads of fun to make them. These are fresh truffles and need to be kept in the refrigerator and consumed within a week—that's if you can resist eating them right away!

**Makes 30**

**Preparation time:** 15 minutes, plus chilling

**Cooking time:** 5 minutes

8 ounces semisweet chocolate, chopped

2 tablespoons milk

1 tablespoon espresso coffee

1 stick unsalted butter, softened

2 egg yolks

¼ cup unsweetened cocoa powder, sifted

Gently melt the chocolate and milk in a heatproof bowl set over a saucepan of barely simmering water, making sure the surface of the water does not touch the bowl.

Remove from the heat and stir in the coffee, butter, and egg yolks until combined. Transfer the mixture to a bowl and let set in the refrigerator for 4 hours.

Place the cocoa powder on a plate. Using a tablespoon, scoop out spoonfuls of the chocolate mixture. Coat your hands in cocoa powder to prevent the mixture from sticking and roll the chocolate mixture between the palms of your hand to form walnut-size balls.

Using a fork, roll the truffles in the cocoa powder to coat. Store the truffles in an airtight container in the refrigerator for up to 1 week. See previous page for the finished result.

## Tip

It is best to remove the truffles from the refrigerator and bring to room temperature before serving.

**1.** Melt the chocolate and milk.

**2.** Off the heat, stir in the coffee, butter, and egg yolks, then let set.

**3.** Scoop out spoonfuls of chocolate mixture and roll into balls.

**4.** Roll the truffles in cocoa powder to coat.

# Pink fizz champagne truffles

If like me you like rosé champagne and chocolate, this after-dinner truffle with extra pop will be your new favorite treat.

**Makes 15**

**Preparation time:** 15 minutes, plus chilling

**Cooking time:** 5 minutes

4 ounces semisweet chocolate, chopped

½ cup light cream

2 teaspoons Marc de Champagne

2 teaspoons plain popping candy

⅓ cup confectioners' sugar

1 teaspoon pink food coloring

Put the chocolate into a heatproof bowl. Put the cream into a small saucepan and heat until steaming hot, but do not let it boil, then pour onto the chocolate and stir gently until melted, smooth, and glossy. Let cool.

When cooled, stir in the champagne, then the popping candy. Let set in the refrigerator for at least 4 hours.

Put the confectioners' sugar and food coloring into a blender and process together. Tip onto a plate.

Using a teaspoon, scoop up the ganache and roll between the palms of your hand to form perfect round shapes. Using a fork, roll the truffles in the pink confectioners' sugar to coat. Store the truffles in an airtight container in the refrigerator for up to 1 week.

## Tip

Dust your hands with confectioners' sugar before rolling the truffles to stop the ganache from sticking.

# Crisp chocolate bonbons

Very crunchy, very nutty, and, of course, very chocolaty; theses treats make a perfect gift wrapped in cellophane wrappers and placed in a beautiful glass jar.

**Makes 24**

**Preparation time:** 15 minutes, plus cooling and chilling

**Cooking time:** 5 minutes

8 ounces milk chocolate, coarsely chopped

1 cup crème fraîche

1¾ cups crispy rice cereal

½ cup roasted and chopped almonds, roasted (see Tip on page 44)

½ cup roasted and chopped hazelnuts (see Tip on page 44)

Line a 7½-inch-square shallow baking pan with parchment paper.

Melt the chocolate in a heatproof bowl set over a saucepan of barely simmering water until smooth and glossy, making sure the surface of the water does not touch the bowl. Meanwhile, put the crème fraîche into a saucepan and heat gently, then stir into the melted chocolate. Let cool.

Divide the chocolate mixture among three small bowls and stir one of the dry ingredients into each.

Spoon the coated crispy rice cereal into the prepared pan and press down with the back of a spoon. Let set in the refrigerator.

Once set, spread the coated almonds over the top, then return to the refrigerator and let set.

Repeat with the hazelnut mixture to form three layers, then cover with plastic wrap and chill in the refrigerator for at least 4 hours, until completely set.

Turn out of the pan onto a cutting board and cut into 24 small rectangles using a large, sharp knife. Wrap the bonbons in candy wrapping paper. Store in an airtight container for up to 1 week.

# Palet d'or

Palet d'or are a chocolatier classic and most good pâtisseries will have some on display in their stores. They are smooth chocolates, flavored with coffee and hazelnut and, as the name suggests, decorated with gold leaf.

**Makes about 60**

**Preparation time:** 45 minutes, plus standing and chilling

**Cooking time:** 10 minutes

## For the ganache

8 ounces semisweet chocolate, coarsely chopped

⅔ cup heavy cream

2 teaspoons coffee extract

2½ teaspoons light corn syrup

2 tablespoons hazelnut spread

1½ tablespoons unsalted butter

1 teaspoon vanilla paste or extract

## For the coating

10 ounces semisweet chocolate, finely chopped

few sheets of edible gold leaf or chocolate transfer acetate sheet with a gold design

To make the ganache, melt the chocolate in a large heatproof bowl set over a saucepan of barely simmering water, making sure the surface of the water does not touch the bowl.

Put the cream into a small saucepan and heat until steaming hot, but do not let it boil. Stir in the coffee extract, then let cool for a few minutes. Stir the cooled cream into the melted chocolate until smooth and glossy. Gently stir in the corn syrup, hazelnut spread, butter, and vanilla. Let stand for a couple of hours, stirring occasionally to prevent the mixture from separating.

Line an 8-inch-square, shallow baking pan with parchment paper. Spread the ganache about ¾ inch thick in the pan and smooth over the top using a spatula. Cover with plastic wrap and let set in the refrigerator for at least 2 hours.

When ready to coat, melt, cool, and reheat the semisweet chocolate following the Tempering technique on page 12. If using, crumble the gold leaf all over a sheet of acetate.

Carefully turn out the ganache onto a cutting board and cut into ¾-inch squares using a large, sharp knife. Using a fork, dip each one into the tempered chocolate to completely coat, tapping off any excess, then carefully place on the prepared acetate sheet. Before the chocolates set completely, cover with another sheet of acetate, smoothing it gently. Let set in the refrigerator.

When set, carefully remove the chocolates from the acetate sheets and place, gold side up, in a beautiful box or on a serving tray. Store in a cool, dry place for up to 1 week.

# Chocolate-coated cherries

These delicate cherries soaked in brandy and coated with chocolate are to die for, but they are not for the faint-hearted, because the alcohol contained in them is strong!

**Makes about 60**

**Preparation time:** 2 hours, plus 2 months marinating, setting, and resting

**Cooking time:** 10 minutes

confectioners' sugar, for dusting

⅓ cup chocolate sprinkles

10 ounces white ready-to-use rolled fondant (available from a cake decorating shop or online)

12 ounces semisweet chocolate, finely chopped

**For the cherries**

1 pound fresh cherries with stems, washed and dried

⅔ cup granulated sugar

2 cinnamon sticks

2 teaspoons vanilla paste or extract

6 coriander seeds, crushed

2 cups Cognac

To marinate the cherries, pack the fruit tightly into a sterilized 1-quart canning jar (see Tip on page 164), alternating each layer of fruit with a sprinkle of sugar. Push in the cinnamon sticks, vanilla, and coriander. Cover completely with the brandy up to ½ inch from the top of the jar and seal. Place the jar in a hot water bath and process for 10 minutes if you live below 1,000 feet (for more details, refer to a book on canning or search online for the National Center for Home Food Preservation). Let soak for two months in a dark, cool, dry place. Gently shake the jar every 2–3 weeks so the sugar dissolves. Alternatively, keep the cherries in the refrigerator for 2 weeks.

Drain the cherries (reserve the brandy for later use), and pat dry with paper towels. Line a baking sheet with parchment paper and dust generously with confectioners' sugar. Place the sprinkles in a shallow bowl.

Melt the fondant in a small saucepan until liquid and hot (122°F on a candy thermometer, if you have one). Dip the cherries into the fondant, using the stems, and place on the prepared sheet. Let cool and set.

Melt, cool, and reheat the chocolate following the Tempering technique on page 12.

Using the stems, dip each cherry into the tempered chocolate, making sure that one-quarter of the stem is coated to seal the fruit completely. Carefully shake off any excess chocolate. Dip the bottoms into the sprinkles before placing on a sheet of parchment paper. Let set, then put into a sterilized airtight container. Let stand for 1 week in the refrigerator before eating—by that time the fondant will have melted and transformed into alcoholic syrup.

## Tip

The fondant must still be white when it has melted— if it is clear, it is too hot and needs to cool before use.

# Large hazelnut bouchées

Bouchées are large chocolate treats, which you usually graze on throughout the day, making the indulgent pleasure last even longer.

**Makes 36**

**Preparation time:** 30 minutes, plus cooling, chilling, and setting

**Cooking time:** 20 minutes

**For the filling**

1 cup hazelnuts

⅔ cup granulated sugar

butter, for greasing

3 ounces milk chocolate, coarsely chopped

1 ounces semisweet chocolate, coarsely chopped

**For the coating**

4 ounces semisweet chocolate, coarsely chopped

4 ounces milk chocolate, coarsely chopped

¼ cup toasted and chopped almonds (see Tip on page 44)

a couple of pinches of coarse sea salt crystals

First make the filling. Preheat the oven to 350°F. Place the hazelnuts on a baking sheet and roast in the oven for 10 minutes, until lightly golden.

Meanwhile, put the sugar into a heavy saucepan and heat until it forms a dark caramel, then stir in the roasted hazelnuts and turn onto a greased baking sheet. Let cool completely.

When cool, break the brittle into smaller pieces and place in a blender, then process to a fine powder.

Melt the milk chocolate and semisweet chocolate in a heatproof bowl set over a saucepan of barely simmering water, making sure the surface of the water does not touch the bowl. Remove from the heat and stir in the hazelnut powder, mixing to a smooth, thick paste.

Using a teaspoon, fill a silicone round-shape chocolate mold with the mixture and let set in the refrigerator. When completely set, carefully remove the chocolates from the molds. (The filling makes about 36 chocolates, so you may have to make these in batches.)

To coat the bouchées, melt both chocolates in a heatproof bowl as above, then remove from the heat and stir in the almonds and salt. Using a fork, dip the chocolate balls into the melted chocolate to coat completely, tapping off any excess. Place on a sheet of parchment paper or acetate and let set. Store in an airtight container for up to 1 week.

# Honey and milk chocolate bars

Kids are usually fonder of milk and white chocolate, so what could be more fun than making your own treats before eating them? This easy-to-make recipe will be a hit with adults, too.

**Serves 8**

**Preparation time:** 10 minutes, plus chilling

**Cooking time:** 10 minutes

7 ounces milk chocolate, coarsely chopped, plus an extra 1 ounce for the topping

3 tablespoons unsalted butter, plus extra for greasing

2 tablespoons honey

2 tablespoons condensed milk

2⅔ cups crispy rice cereal

⅓ cup dry coconut

5 ounces white chocolate, coarsely chopped

Grease a 7-inch-square, shallow baking pan and line with parchment paper.

Put the milk chocolate, butter, honey, and condensed milk into a small saucepan and heat gently until melted and smooth, then stir in the crispy rice cereal and coconut.

Spoon the mixture into the prepared pan and level the top with the back of a spoon. Let set in the refrigerator for at least 30 minutes.

Melt the white chocolate in a heatproof bowl set over a saucepan of barely simmering water, making sure the surface of the water does not touch the bowl. Let cool for a few minutes, then spread over the top of the rice cake. Return to the refrigerator to set.

Melt the remaining 1 ounce of milk chocolate as above, then spoon the chocolate into a small disposable pastry bag with a small hole snipped at the tip. Drizzle a pattern over the white chocolate and let set at room temperature.

Turn out of the pan onto a cutting board and cut into rectangular bars using a large, sharp knife. Store in an airtight container or wrap in cellophane bags for gifts.

## Tip

This is an easy recipe for kids to make, but it will require adult supervision and help, especially when cutting the cake into bars with the sharp knife!

# Mint chocolate squares

After-dinner mints have always been the perfect way to finish a meal when served with strong coffee or infusions. These little square ones will become a favorite.

**Makes 36**

**Preparation time:** 10 minutes, plus chilling

**Cooking time:** 10 minutes

butter, for greasing

12 ounces semisweet chocolate, coarsely chopped

2⅔ cups confectioners' sugar

1 tablespoon vegetable oil

2 tablespoons milk

¼ teaspoon peppermint extract

Grease an 8-inch-square, 2½-inch deep baking pan. Line the bottom and sides with parchment paper, letting it hang over the sides.

Melt the chocolate in a heatproof bowl set over a saucepan of barely simmering water, making sure the surface of the water does not touch the bowl. Spread half of the melted chocolate over the bottom of the prepared pan and smooth using a small spatula. Chill for 15 minutes, or until set.

Sift the confectioners' sugar into a heatproof bowl, then stir in the oil and milk to form a thick paste. Place the bowl over a saucepan of simmering water and heat for a few minutes, stirring. Stir in the peppermint, then let cool for 2 minutes.

Pour the peppermint mixture over the chocolate in the pan, spreading with a spatula. Return to the refrigerator for 15 minutes, or until just set.

Cover the peppermint layer with the remaining melted chocolate, then make a wave pattern on the top using a fork. Chill in the refrigerator for at least 1 hour.

Carefully lift out of the pan onto a cutting board and cut into 36 small squares using a large, warm knife. Store in an airtight container for up to 1 week.

## Tip

If the peppermint mixture is too thick once cooled for 2 minutes, add an extra 1 teaspoon of milk at a time to loosen.

# Lapsang souchong pralines

Chocolate works with so many flavors and that's why chocolatiers are having a ball creating confections using extraordinary scents. The smoky flavor of the lapsang souchong tea is a perfect example.

**Makes 24**

**Preparation time:** 15 minutes, plus cooling and chilling

**Cooking time:** 10 minutes

5 ounces semisweet chocolate, coarsely chopped

⅔ cup heavy cream

2 tablespoons loose leaf lapsang souchong tea

2 tablespoons packed dark brown sugar

2 teaspoons vanilla paste or extract

8 tablespoons unsweetened cocoa powder

Melt the chocolate in a heatproof bowl set over a saucepan of barely simmering water, making sure the surface of the water does not touch the bowl. Remove from the heat.

Put the cream, tea, and sugar into a small saucepan and bring to a gentle simmer over low heat. Let cool and steep for 4–5 minutes.

Pass the cream mixture through a fine strainer into a bowl. Stir in the vanilla, then pour it over the melted chocolate and stir until smooth and glossy. Let cool and set to a piping consistency.

Line a baking sheet with parchment paper. Spoon the mixture into a pastry bag fitted with a ¾-inch diameter plain piping tip, then pipe long lengths onto the prepared baking sheet. Let set in the refrigerator.

When solid, cut the lengths into 2-inch oblong sticks using a sharp knife. Sift the cocoa powder into a shallow bowl, then roll the sticks in the cocoa to coat. Place on a serving plate or in a gift box.

# Chocolate guimauve

Marshmallows have made a huge comeback and are no longer just for kids. Gourmet mallows are everywhere and these chocolate ones are definitely for grown-ups.

**Makes 45 squares**

**Preparation time:** 25 minutes, plus chilling

**Cooking time:** 10 minutes

⅔ cup unsweetened cocoa powder

⅔ cup water

2 teaspoons amaretto liqueur

1 cup granulated sugar

2 tablespoons gelatin powder

2 teaspoons vanilla paste

½ cup light corn syrup

4 ounces semisweet chocolate, coarsely chopped

Line an 8-inch-square, 2½-inch-deep baking pan with parchment paper, then dust generously with some of the cocoa powder.

Put the water, amaretto, sugar, and gelatin powder into a small saucepan over low heat and stir until it has dissolved, but do not let it boil. Remove from the heat and stir in the vanilla paste.

Transfer the mixture to the bowl of a freestanding mixer, add the corn syrup, and beat to stiff peaks—this may take up to 12 minutes.

Meanwhile, melt the chocolate in a heatproof bowl set over a saucepan of barely simmering water, making sure the surface of the water does not touch the bowl. Let cool for a few minutes, then fold into the whisked mallow.

Pour the mixture into the prepared pan and spread level using a damp spatula. Let set in the refrigerator for at least 1 hour.

Dust a cutting board with some more of the cocoa powder and sift the remaining cocoa powder into a shallow bowl. Turn out the mallow onto the board, then cut into bite-size cubes. Using a fork, roll the mallows in the sifted cocoa powder, shaking off the excess. Store in an airtight container for up to 2 weeks.

# Chocolate honeycomb toffee

I love offering shards of honeycomb toffee (sponge candy) as gifts wrapped up in cellophane. They are great on their own or crumbled on ice cream.

**Makes 1 (8-inch) square**
**Preparation time:** 10 minutes, plus setting
**Cooking time:** 8 minutes

unsalted butter, for greasing
1 cup granulated sugar
¼ cup light corn syrup
1 ounce semisweet chocolate, finely chopped
1 tablespoon baking soda

Grease an 8-inch-square shallow baking pan.

Melt the sugar and light corn syrup in a heavy saucepan over low heat, then increase the heat to medium and simmer for 3–4 minutes, or until the mixture is thick and a dark caramel color.

Remove from the heat, add the chocolate, and immediately whisk in the baking soda so that the mixture froths up—stand back just in case.

Pour the mixture into the prepared pan and let set at room temperature for about 2–3 hours.

Remove from the pan and break into large pieces using a rolling pin. Store in cellophane bags for up to 1 week.

## Tip

To make the honeycomb toffee more luxurious, drizzle some melted white and milk chocolates on the top of the pieces before serving or wrapping them.

# Chocolate fudge

I had never come across fudge before I arrived in the UK, but it didn't take me long to become fond of these candies, eaten mostly on trips to seaside towns. They make such a great gift when beautifully wrapped.

**Makes 36**

**Preparation time:** 10 minutes, plus chilling

**Cooking time:** 5 minutes

13 ounces semisweet chocolate, coarsely chopped

1 (14-ounce) can condensed milk

2 tablespoons unsalted butter, plus extra for greasing

¾ cup confectioners' sugar

Lightly grease a 7½-inch-square shallow baking pan.

Put the chocolate, condensed milk, and butter into a small saucepan and melt gently over low heat, stirring occasionally, until smooth and silky. Sift in the confectioners' sugar and mix thoroughly.

Press the mixture into the prepared pan and smooth over the top with the back of a spoon. Cover with plastic wrap and let set in the refrigerator for 1 hour.

Turn out the fudge onto a cutting board and cut into 36 squares. Store in an airtight container in a cool, dry place for up to 1 week.

## Tip

For variety, try adding chopped nuts or dried fruits to the mixture.

# Chocolate orange truffles

When you hear about the popular combination of chocolate and orange, you always think semisweet chocolate, but it does work surprisingly well with white chocolate, too, if not better.

**Makes 24**

**Preparation time:** 40 minutes, plus chilling and setting

**Cooking time:** 8 minutes

⅓ cup heavy cream

1 pound white chocolate, chopped

2 tablespoons unsalted butter

4 teaspoons orange liqueur

¼ cup candied orange peel, finely chopped

2 ounces semisweet chocolate, coarsely chopped

Put the cream into a small saucepan and heat to just below boiling point. Stir in half of the white chocolate and the butter until smooth. Add the liqueur and orange peel, then transfer the mixture to a bowl and refrigerate until firm.

Line a baking sheet with parchment paper. Using a teaspoon, scoop up small amounts of the ganache, shape into balls with your hands, and place on the baking sheet.

Melt the remaining white chocolate in a heatproof bowl set over a saucepan of barely simmering water, making sure the surface of the water does not touch the bowl. Let cool for a few minutes.

Using a fork, dip each ganache ball into the melted white chocolate, then return to the lined baking sheet and let set.

Melt the semisweet chocolate as above and let cool for a few minutes. Spoon the melted semisweet chocolate into a small pastry bag fitted with a thin piping tip, then pipe fine lines onto each truffle and let set. Store the truffles in an airtight container in a cool, dry place for up to 1 week.

## Tip

If the balls of ganache soften before you are ready to dip them in the melted white chocolate, place them in the refrigerator until firm, or place them in the freezer for 10 minutes.

# Soft chocolate caramel

Brittany, where I grew up, is the only region of France that uses salted butter for everyday use. Caramel is one of those candies that work so well with a little salt added, too.

**Makes 25**

**Preparation time:** 20 minutes, plus setting overnight

**Cooking time:** 20 minutes

oil, for greasing

2 ounces bittersweet chocolate, 99 percent cocoa solids or the darkest you can get, coarsely chopped

4 teaspoons water

⅓ cup light corn syrup

1¼ cups superfine sugar

1 stick salted butter

1 cup heavy cream

Lightly oil an 8-inch-square shallow baking pan.

Melt the chocolate in a heatproof bowl set over a saucepan of barely simmering water, making sure the surface of the water does not touch the bowl.

Meanwhile, place the water, corn syrup, and sugar in a heavy saucepan and heat over medium heat until it forms a nice blond caramel. Remove from the heat and add 1 tablespoon of the butter to cool the mixture.

Put the cream into a small saucepan and heat slightly, then slowly pour it into the caramel, stirring gently. Add the remaining butter, return the saucepan to the heat, and heat until the mixture reaches 244°F on a candy thermometer.

Remove from the heat and stir in the melted chocolate until smooth. Pour into the prepared pan and let cool and set at room temperature overnight.

Turn out the caramel onto a cutting board and cut into 25 small squares using a large knife. The caramels look nice stored in a jar or wrapped in colorful paper wrappers.

Spicy "Aztec" hot chocolate

# Drinks, Spreads & Sauces

# Spicy "Aztec" hot chocolate

This is probably the oldest known hot chocolate recipe. The Aztecs used this spicy drink to give them power when going into battle. The combination of the semisweet chocolate and spices makes it a real pick-me-up elixir— drink this and you will be ready to face any battle!

**Serves 4**

**Preparation time:** 5 minutes

**Cooking time:** 5 minutes

4 cups milk

4 ounces semisweet chocolate, coarsely chopped

2 tablespoons packed light brown sugar

1 teaspoon ground cinnamon

1 teaspoon freshly grated nutmeg

1 teaspoon ground black pepper

½ cup heavy cream

ground cinnamon and freshly grated nutmeg, for dusting

Put the milk into a heavy saucepan and bring to a boil. Reduce the heat, then add the chocolate, sugar, and spices.

Using a small wire whisk, whisk until the chocolate has completely melted. Simmer for 1 minute, then remove from the heat and whisk in the cream.

Pour into tall mugs and serve with a dusting of cinnamon and grated nutmeg. See previous page for the finished result.

**1.** Heat the milk and add the chocolate.

**2.** Add the sugar.

**3.** Then add the spices and whisk until the chocolate has melted.

**4.** Remove from the heat and whisk in the cream.

**5.** Pour into mugs.

**6.** Serve with a dusting of cinnamon and a grating of nutmeg.

# Chocolate martini

There is something about starting an evening with a martini cocktail. This chocolate version will surprise and amaze your guests, but watch out because it is a smooth and easy-to-drink concoction.

**Serves 1**

**Preparation time:** 5 minutes, plus chilling

1 tablespoon finely grated semisweet chocolate

¼ cup heavy cream

1½ shots (¼ cup) Irish cream liqueur

1½ shots (¼ cup) crème de cacao

½ shot (4 teaspoons) vodka

ice cubes

First prepare your Manhattan glass. Using your fingertip, wet the rim of the glass with water. Sprinkle the grated chocolate on a small plate and turn the glass in the chocolate, making sure the rim is coated with chocolate. Chill in the refrigerator and reserve the remaining chocolate.

When ready to serve, lightly whip the cream until thickened slightly but still sloppy. Put all the alcohol into a cocktail shaker with some ice cubes. Shake well, then pour it into the prepared chilled glass and add a twirl of the cream. Finish with a sprinkle of the reserved chocolate and serve immediately. Santé!

# Chocolate and caramel cocktail

This is one of my favorite winter cocktails to serve to friends. It needs a little effort, but the good news is it can be prepared in advance. Be careful, however, it is hard to stop at one—drink in moderation.

**Serves 3–4**

**Preparation time:** 10 minutes, plus chilling

**Cooking time:** 5 minutes

3 tablespoons unsweetened cocoa powder, plus 1 teaspoon

1 teaspoon sugar syrup

¼ cup granulated sugar

4 teaspoons water

1 cup light cream

¼ cup crème de cacao

¼ cup orange liqueur

ice cubes

First prepare your glasses. Place the 1 teaspoon of cocoa powder and sugar syrup on separate saucers. Dip the rim of each glass into the syrup and then into the cocoa powder. Chill in the refrigerator.

Put the sugar and water into a heavy saucepan and heat gently until the sugar has dissolved, then increase the heat and cook until it forms a nice dark blond caramel color. Add the cream and whisk in, using a wire whisk, scraping up the caramel from the bottom of the pan. Add the remaining cocoa powder and cook for another 2 minutes, or until the mixture is smooth.

Pass through a strainer into a blender to remove any pieces of caramel, then add both liqueurs and blend for few minutes. Chill in the refrigerator.

When ready to serve, place some ice cubes in a cocktail shaker with the chilled cocktail and shake well. Pass it through a cocktail strainer, pour into the chilled glasses, and serve immediately. Let's get the party started!

# Double chocolate milk shake

This version of a classic chocolate milk shake reminds me of the first time I ate in a diner in the United States and had my first milk shake. A good shake should be creamy, thick, and smooth, and leave you full—it's almost a dessert in a glass.

**Serves 4**

**Preparation time:** 5 minutes, plus chilling

**Cooking time:** 3 minutes

4 cups milk

4 ounces semisweet chocolate, coarsely chopped

4 large scoops of good-quality chocolate ice cream

2 teaspoons chocolate extract

2 tablespoons malted milk powder

20 ice cubes

good-quality hot cocoa mix, for dusting

Chill four tall serving glasses in the refrigerator.

Put the milk into a saucepan and heat to simmering point. Remove from the heat, add the chocolate, and stir until completely melted. Let cool, then chill in the refrigerator for 10 minutes.

Pour the chocolate milk into a blender with the remaining ingredients. Blend at full speed until the mixture is light and frothy and there are no more ice crystals.

Pour into the chilled glasses, dust generously with the hot cocoa mix, and serve immediately. Sit back and enjoy.

# Chocolate and cola float

This is a reminder of those great soda parlors where as kids we were treated to fabulous Sunday outings. For me, the best treat was the cola float, because we never drank cola at home, so it was a double celebration! I wish soda parlors would make a comeback. In the meantime, try this recipe.

**Serves 4**

**Preparation time:** 10 minutes, plus chilling

1 cup heavy cream

4 cups cola (preferrably the old-fashion type)

2 teaspoons vanilla extract or paste

8 scoops of good-quality chocolate ice cream

½ cup maraschino cherries, plus a few extra to decorate

1 ounce semisweet chocolate, grated

Chill four tall sundae glasses in the refrigerator.

When ready to serve, lightly whip the cream until thickened slightly but still sloppy. Put to one side.

Put the cola, vanilla, ice cream, and cherries into a large blender, in two batches, if necessary, and use the pulse button to blend together.

Pour into the chilled glasses, spoon the cream on top, and sprinkle with the grated chocolate. Decorate with a few maraschino cherries for a little touch of kitsch and serve immediately.

## Tip

It is best to use the pulse button when blending the cola float, because it will fizz and froth a lot.

# Conquistadors' hot cocoa

The conquistadors were responsible for introducing cocoa to Europe, and this version of hot chocolate is also known as Spanish chocolate. I've added some Seville orange to it for an Iberian touch. This rich drink is best served with churros, the Spanish doughnuts. However, a warning—you can get hooked!

**Serves 6–8**
**Preparation time:** 5 minutes
**Cooking time:** 10 minutes

1 cup water
½ cup packed light brown sugar
2 tablespoons cornstarch
1 cup unsweetened cocoa powder
2 cups milk
grated zest of 1 orange
(Seville if in season)
1 teaspoon vanilla paste or extract
1 teaspoon pure orange extract
(optional)

Put the water and sugar into a heavy saucepan and bring to a boil, stirring until the sugar has completely dissolved. Remove from the heat, sift together the cornstarch and cocoa powder, and whisk into the syrup using a small wire whisk.

Return the pan to the heat and cook until the mixture forms a thick paste. Add the milk a little at a time, whisking continuously until smooth and glossy, then add the grated orange zest, vanilla, and orange extract, if using. Simmer for 5 minutes, stirring continuously.

Serve piping hot in small, warm coffee cups.

## Tip

For a grown-up version, replace the orange extract with orange liqueur.

# After-dinner mint hot chocolate

I know it is more typical to serve after-dinner mint chocolates, but why not serve a hot mint chocolate instead to impress your guests? It's one of my favorite dinner party treats. I'm sure you and your friends will love it, too.

**Serves 14–16**
**Preparation time:** 10 minutes
**Cooking time:** 10 minutes

1 cup packed light brown sugar
4 ounces hard mint candies
2 cups water
1½ cups unsweetened cocoa powder
2 tablespoons cornstarch
2 cups milk

Place the sugar and mint candies in a food processor and blend to a fine powder. Put the water and sugar powder into a heavy saucepan and bring to a boil, stirring, until the sugar powder has dissolved. Remove from the heat, sift together the cocoa powder and cornstarch, and whisk into the syrup using a small wire whisk.

Return the pan to the heat and simmer until the mixture forms a smooth paste. Add the milk a little at a time, whisking until the mixture is smooth and glossy. Serve immediately in small, heatproof shot glasses.

# Proper Italian hot chocolate

When growing up, my family always went skiing during the festive seasons. We went to a small ski resort a few miles from Turin and our treat was this phenomenal thick hot chocolate called *cioccolata calda*. The legend goes: "If your spoon doesn't stand up in your cup, it is not a proper one," but even I haven't managed to get mine to that legendary status!

**Serves 6–8**
**Preparation time:** 5 minutes
**Cooking time:** 15 minutes

4 cups milk
½ cup packed light brown sugar
1 cup plus 3 tablespoons unsweetened cocoa powder
⅔ cup crème fraîche
2 teaspoons vanilla paste or extract

Put the milk and sugar into a heavy saucepan and heat gently until the sugar has dissolved. Remove from the heat and whisk in the cocoa powder and crème fraîche.

Return to low heat and bring to a simmer, stirring. Simmer for about 10 minutes, or until thickened. Add the vanilla and whisk until frothy. Serve in small, warm cups.

# Mocha brûlée

This extraordinary drink is a fantastic party piece that needs a little preparation, but is worth all the effort.

**Serves 4**
**Preparation time:** 10 minutes
**Cooking time:** 5 minutes

3⅓ cups milk

4 shots of espresso coffee
made with 1 cup just-boiled water

½ cup good-quality hot cocoa mix

2 teaspoons vanilla paste or extract

¼ cup demerara sugar
or other raw sugar

Put the milk into a saucepan and heat to just below boiling point.

Put the coffee into a heatproof bowl, add the cocoa mix, and stir until blended. Using a small wire whisk, add 2½ cups of the hot milk, a little at a time, until the mixture is smooth. Stir in the vanilla, then pour into four warm, flameproof coffee cups or small mugs.

Using an electric milk frother, froth the remaining hot milk. Spoon on top of the coffees and level it flat with a knife. Sprinkle the sugar over the froth in each glass and caramelize using a kitchen blowtorch. Serve immediately.

## Tip

Skim milk froths more easily than low-fat or whole milk.

# Viennese chocolate

Vienna is known as the world capital of the coffee shop, where for hundreds of years they've served specialty coffee, pastries, and other hot drinks. Viennese chocolate is certainly one of their most famous treats—pure indulgence in a glass.

**Serves 4**

**Preparation time:** 10 minutes

**Cooking time:** 10 minutes

8 ounces semisweet chocolate, coarsely chopped

½ cup heavy cream

3 tablespoons confectioners' sugar

2 teaspoons vanilla sugar

4 cups milk

¼ cup firmly packed light brown sugar

unsweetened cocoa powder and ground cinnamon, for dusting

Melt the chocolate in a heatproof bowl set over a saucepan of barely simmering water, making sure the surface of the water does not touch the bowl.

Meanwhile, whip the cream, confectioners' sugar, and vanilla sugar to stiff peaks and put to one side.

Put the milk and brown sugar into a saucepan and heat gently until the sugar has dissolved. Whisk in the melted chocolate a little at the time, then whisk over low heat for at least 5 minutes, or until the mixture is smooth and glossy.

Pour the hot chocolate into four tall, warm latte glasses. Scoop the cream high on top, lightly dust with cocoa powder and cinnamon, and serve immediately.

# Hazelnut and chocolate spread

You can never beat homemade products, and this spread is the absolute proof. It's a perfect breakfast treat spread generously on toasted brioche, and it's also a great gift idea when presented in beautiful jars.

**Makes two (1-pint) jars**

**Preparation time:** 5 minutes, plus cooling

**Cooking time:** 10 minutes

1 cup ground hazelnuts

5 ounces semisweet chocolate, coarsely chopped

2 sticks unsalted butter

2 teaspoons vanilla paste or extract

1 (14-ounce) can condensed milk

2 tablespoons hazelnut oil

Preheat the oven to 350°F. Spread the ground hazelnuts on a baking sheet and roast for 3–4 minutes, or until a nice rich golden color and the full aroma escapes from the oven. Let cool.

Melt the chocolate and one-quarter of the butter in a small heatproof bowl set over a saucepan of barely simmering water, making sure the surface of the water does not touch the bowl. When melted, remove the pan from the heat but keep the bowl over the hot water. Stir in the roasted hazelnuts and the remaining ingredients until the mixture is smooth and glossy.

Pour into two sterilized 1-pint jars (see Tip below), then let cool completely before sealing with the lids. Store in the refrigerator for up to 2 weeks. This is best removed from the refrigerator 1 hour before serving.

# White chocolate spread

This rich, luxurious white chocolate spread is easy to put together. It is the perfect accompaniment to toasted gingerbread or malt loaf.

**Makes about 1¼ cups**

**Preparation time:** 5 minutes

**Cooking time:** 5 minutes

8 ounces white chocolate, coarsely chopped

⅔ cup canned condensed milk

2 teaspoons vanilla paste

¼ cup light cream

Melt all the ingredients until smooth and glossy in a large heatproof bowl set over a saucepan of barely simmering water, making sure the surface of the water does not touch the bowl.

Pour into small, sterilized jars (see Tip below), then let cool completely before sealing with the lids. Store in the refrigerator for up to 2 weeks.

## Tip

To sterilize jars, put clean, washed, and dried jars into a cold oven with the lids off. Heat the oven to 350°F, keeping the jars in the oven for 20 minutes. Pour your chocolate spread into the jars while still warm from the oven.

# Chocolate fondue

I know fondue is out of date, but a good chocolate fondue is a great alternative to a dessert or perfect for a party. You can be as creative as you want with the food to be dipped.

**Serves 6**

**Preparation time:** 15 minutes

**Cooking time:** 5 minutes

10 ounces semisweet chocolate, coarsely chopped

2 tablespoons milk

1 cup heavy cream

6 tablespoons unsalted butter, softened

1 teaspoon ground cinnamon

1 teaspoon vanilla paste or extract

2 tablespoons dark rum

**For dipping and coating**

3 bananas, cut into chunky pieces

3 ripe pears, peeled, cored, and cut into chunky pieces

juice of 1 lemon

12 large marshmallows

assortment of dried fruit, such as figs, dates, and prunes

1⅓ cups roasted and chopped hazelnuts (see Tip on page 44)

2 cups flaked dry coconut

First, prepare the dips. Toss the bananas and pears with the lemon juice to prevent them from browning. Arrange the prepared fruit, marshmallows, and dried fruit on a large platter or in ramekins, together with the roasted nuts and coconut. Make a pile of metal or wooden kebab sticks on the side.

To make the fondue, place a fondue pan in a bain-marie. Alternatively, place a heatproof serving bowl over a saucepan of simmering water. Add the chocolate and milk and melt together, then whisk in the cream. Keep warm, then just before serving stir in the butter, cinnamon, vanilla, and rum.

Take the warm fondue to the table hot and encourage people to help themselves. Use the kebab sticks to dip the fruits and marshmallows into the hot chocolate, then roll into the nuts or coconut. A fun way to end a dinner party!

# Four ultimate chocolate sauces

Chocolate sauces are a perfect accompaniment to desserts, crepes, waffles, and ice cream. Here I've penned four of my favorite ones.

## Semisweet chocolate sauce

**Makes 2 cups**
**Preparation time:** 5 minutes
**Cooking time:** 2 minutes

½ cup milk
½ cup light cream
¼ cup granulated sugar
8 ounces semisweet chocolate, chopped
4 tablespoons unsalted butter, softened

Put the milk, cream, and sugar into a saucepan and heat gently until the sugar has dissolved. Remove from the heat and add the chocolate, stirring until melted. Stir in the butter. Serve warm on ice cream or over cream puffs, or chill, then serve with cake or crepes.

## Irish cream chocolate sauce

Make the semisweet chocolate sauce as above, stirring in 3 tablespoons Irish cream liqueur after adding the butter.

# Zesty white chocolate sauce

**Makes about 1¼ cups**
**Preparation time:** 5 minutes
**Cooking time:** 2 minutes

⅔ cup light cream
¼ cup milk
8 ounces white chocolate, chopped
grated zest of 1 lemon
1 tablespoon extra virgin olive oil

Put the cream and milk into a saucepan and bring to a boil. Remove from the heat and stir in the chocolate until melted and smooth, then stir in the lemon zest and olive oil. This superb combination is perfect for fruity, summery desserts.

# Milk chocolate and hazelnut sauce

**Makes about 1¼ cups**
**Preparation time:** 5 minutes
**Cooking time:** 5 minutes

8 ounces milk chocolate,
coarsely chopped
⅓ cup light cream
1 teaspoon vanilla extract
2 teaspoond honey
¼ cup ground hazelnuts, roasted
(see Tip on page 44)

Melt the chocolate in a heatproof bowl set over a saucepan of barely simmering water, making sure the surface of the water does not touch the bowl. Stir in the cream, vanilla, and honey until smooth and glossy, then stir in the ground hazelnuts. Serve warm over ice cream, pancakes, or fruit.

# Chocolate glaze

This is the perfect recipe to spread over baked goods such as brownies and cakes. The easy glaze is rich, smooth, and glossy, so it works well as a paint for those of you ready to express your artistic flair on fruit, plates, or body parts!

**Makes** 2/3 cup

**Preparation time:** 2 minutes

**Cooking time:** 3 minutes

4 ounces semisweet chocolate, coarsely chopped

4 tablespoons unsalted butter

1 tablespoon light corn syrup

1 teaspoon vanilla extract or paste

Melt the chocolate, butter, and light corn syrup in a heatproof bowl set over a saucepan of barely simmering water, making sure the surface of the water does not touch the bowl. Stir occasionally, until smooth and glossy, then add the vanilla.

Using a spatula, spread the glaze over cakes or brownies.

## Tip

If you are feeling artistic, decorate fruit and plates (or body parts!) with the chocolate glaze using a fine, clean paintbrush.

# Index

## Author acknowledgements

# Author's acknowledgments

This book wouldn't have happened without the continuous support of Denise Bates and her team at Mitchell Beazley. A big thank you to Alison Starling for bringing together the "A" team and making sure than the long process to create this book went smoothly with a fabulous end result. All the way through the book my recipes are showcased and styled in a beautiful way to still look accessible with a wicked indulgent side! As with the last three books, Juliette and Sybella have done a fantastic job with both the design and deciphering my bad English. The combination of their talents, as well as the gorgeous photography from the talented Kate Whitaker and styling by Liz Belton, make this book really stand out.

This is my first book featuring a single, main ingredient, and I must thank both Wendy Lee, my food economist, for testing all the recipes, and Rachel Wood, for helping me recreate them for the photo shoot … sorry girls, if I've put you off chocolate for a while! I am sure your taste for it will be back soon. As usual, we had a great time working together and much laughter; we all deserved that homemade fried chicken with vintage champagne we all shared together on the last day.

Time to thank, too, the team I call Team Eric: Annie, my agent, Jean, my publicist, and my team at Cake Boy for their continuous support and help. Many thanks to Fiona at Mitchell Beazley and Liz at Hachette USA for their belief and hard work to promote this gorgeous book, of which I am very proud.

A bientot pour le prochain livre!

Eric ✗